SO-AML-730

Guardian Angel
Guardian Devil

A series of short stories describing

GUARDIANSHIP FOR

The **SENIOR** who is too frail to care for himself

The comatose **ACCIDENT VICTIM**

The **MENTALLY ILL**

The **MINOR CHILD** whose
parents are deceased or incapacitated

The **DEVELOPMENTALLY DISABLED ADULT**

AND
HOW TO AVOID GUARDIANSHIP
IN EACH OF THESE CASES

New Hanover County Public Library
201 Chestnut Street
Wilmington, North Carolina 28401

AMELIA E. POHL, ESQ.

 EAGLE PUBLISHING COMPANY OF BOCA

Copyright © 2009 by AMELIA E. POHL

All rights reserved. No part of this book may be reproduced or transmitted for any purpose, in any form and by any means, graphic, electronic or mechanical, including photocopying, recording, or by any information storage or retrieval system, without permission in writing from AMELIA E. POHL.

The purpose of this book is to provide the reader with an informative overview of the subject; but laws change frequently and are subject to different interpretations as courts rule on the meaning or effect of a law. This book is sold with the understanding that neither the author, nor editors, nor publisher, nor distributors of this book are engaging in, or rendering, legal, accounting, financial planning, medical, psychological counseling or any other professional service.

Pursuant to Internal Revenue Service guidance, be advised that any federal tax advice in this publication was not intended or written to be used, and it cannot be used, by any person or entity for the purpose of avoiding penalties imposed under the Internal Revenue Code (IRS Circular 230 Disclaimer). If you need legal, accounting, financial planning, medical, mental health counseling or any other expert advice, you should seek the services of a licensed professional.

This book is intended for use by the consumer for his or her own benefit. Using this book to counsel someone about the law, tax, medical or mental health matters, may be considered to be an unlicensed and illegal practice.

EAGLE PUBLISHING COMPANY OF BOCA
4199 N. Dixie Highway, #2
Boca Raton, FL   33431
E-mail: info@eaglepublishing.com

Printed in the United States of America ISBN 1-932464-32-8
Library of Congress Catalog Card Number 2008902882

Guardian Angel
Guardian Devil

TABLE OF CONTENTS

PART I   THE WARD AND THE GUARDIAN

PART II AVOIDING GUARDIANSHIP

Foreword

In 1965, Norman Dacey wrote a book entitled *How To Avoid Probate*. It became a best seller. Since then, avoiding probate has become part of the collective intelligence. The general public knows that probate is a good thing to avoid. It can be expensive and time consuming. People understand that it is not all that hard to arrange their finances so that their estate is inherited by their loved ones, quickly, and without the need for probate.

People accept the inevitability of death, so avoiding probate is for everyone. Not so with guardianship. People think "I'm fine. I'll never need a guardian. If something happens to me, my family will take care of me." As the examples in this book will show, that may be a costly assumption. If you ever need a guardian, everyone involved gets a piece of your life-savings pie:

- $$ costs paid to the court to process your guardianship

- $$ fees paid to an examining committee sent by the court to determine whether you need a guardian

- $$ fees paid to an attorney appointed by the Court to represent your best interest

- $$ fees paid to the guardian's attorney to establish the guardianship

- $$ the cost of a bond ordered by the court to protect your property

- $$ fees paid to an appraiser to evaluate your property

And this is just to establish the guardianship.

Legal costs continue year after year until you are returned to capacity or die.

Cost is only one of the problems associated with guardianship. Who gets to serve as guardian can become a matter of life or death.

THE TERRI SCHIAVO AFFAIR

One story that is not included in this book is that of Terri Schiavo. People may think the lesson to be learned from that sad story is that everyone should have a Living Will that gives specific directions concerning whether life support systems should, or should not, be used the event that the person is in a persistent vegetative state.

That isn't the only lesson to be learned. The reason Terri Schiavo's husband was able to have his wife's life support systems disconnected was that he was her court appointed guardian. Although his decision was challenged in court, his <u>right</u> to make that decision was never challenged. He was her legal guardian and it was his right to make life and death decisions for Terri. Terri's parents fought for the right to be guardian. If they had been successful in their effort, she might be alive today.

Depending on your perspective of the case, you might think it great that the husband, and not the parents, won the battle to be guardian. But the point is that who gets to be appointed guardian can become a matter of life or death.

Each story in this book explains how a judge decided who is to serve as guardian. You will see that choices made by a judge can be arbitrary and capricious. It doesn't need to be that way. You can take the decision out of the hands of the judicial system, and provide for your own care in the event of your incapacity.

Part II of this book tells you how.

Guardianship Law

Guardianship is regulated by the state. This means that the laws relating to guardianship are set by the state and not the federal government. All states have guardianship laws. The goal of each state legislature is to protect minors and disabled persons who are unable to care for themselves or their property.

This book describes guardianship as it exists today in the United States. There are variations state to state in guardianship terminology and procedures. Where appropriate, those variations are indicated as footnotes and in the glossary.

Although there may be variations in guardianship terminology and procedures, avoiding guardianship is the same state to state. As you will see, it it relatively simple and inexpensive to protect you and your loved ones from having some Court decide that there is a need to appoint a Guardian.

Amelia E. Pohl, Esq.

Before becoming an attorney in 1985, AMELIA E. POHL taught mathematics on both the high school and college level. During her tenure as Associate Professor of Mathematics at Prince George's Community College in Maryland, she wrote several books in the field of mathematics.

Ms. Pohl graduated from Nova Law School in Ft. Lauderdale, Florida and established a successful Elder Law practice in Boca Raton. During her practice of law, Attorney Pohl combined her skills as teacher, author and lawyer to write legal books for the general public. She wrote a series of state specific books entitled *Guiding Those Left Behind* describing all of the legal and practical things a person needs to do when a loved one dies. She wrote another series of books entitled *A Will Is Not Enough* explaining the importance of avoiding probate and protecting assets during ones lifetime. See the end of this book for a description of these books.

Guardian Angel Guardian Devil is the latest book written by Amelia Pohl. This book explains the importance of avoiding guardianship. The format of this book differs from previous books because it is written as a collection of short stories describing the experiences of Ms. Pohl as she practiced law in the field of guardianship.

ACKNOWLEDGMENT

Many thanks to my friends and family members, Fred Adinolfi, Lisa Adinolfi, Paul Adinolfi, Margot Bosche, John Delzio, Louise Lucas, Carol Planthaber, Nancy Simonyi (in alphabetical order) for their encouragement in the writing of this book. Their comments and review of the manuscript was invaluable.

Special thanks to my husband Bill for his love and support in this and all of my other endeavors.

The Organization of the Book

PART I of this book contains seven short stories each giving an example of what happens when someone who is unable to care for himself has not made arrangements for his care.

CHAPTER 1 IS IMPORTANT

Many readers (including the author) like to skip around when reading a book. In this case, it would be a mistake to skip the first chapter. That chapter gives basic definitions associated with guardianship. It sets the stage for later chapters. If you skip the first chapter, you may find later chapters difficult to follow.

PART II of this book explains how to avoid guardianship by revisiting each of the seven stories in PART I and re-writing the chapter so that the main character takes the necessary steps to avoid guardianship.

GLOSSARY

There is a glossary at the end of the book in case you come across a term in the book that is not familiar to you.

FICTITIOUS NAMES AND EVENTS

This book is written in first person singular. That person is the author AMELIA E. POHL. Although she used her life experiences as the basic of these stories, all the names are fictitious, and the events, as portrayed, are fictitious.

Part I
THE WARD
and
THE GUARDIAN

Guardianship is essentially a duality. There is the *Guardian* and there is the *Ward*. The Guardian is appointed by the Court to care for someone who is unable to care for himself and/or his property. The Ward is the person determined by the Court to be in need of a Guardian, and who is protected by state regulation. The Ward could be a minor, or someone who is too ill to care for himself, or his property.

PART I contains seven short stories. Each story tells about a Ward and a Guardian. The story begins with a description of the Ward and the events leading up to a Court determining that he is in need of a Guardian The second part of the story describes the Guardian and his adventures as he becomes enmeshed in the judicial system known as guardianship. For example, Chapter 1 described how an elderly lady, Virginia, becomes the Ward of her brother, Walter. Chapter 1a, is the story of Walter's experiences in his role as Guardian.

PART II takes these same seven stories and shows how guardianship could have been avoided.

The Elderly Ward 1

It had been a few years since Walter Schnelling visited my law office. He looked older than when I saw him last. Thinner, more bent over. His forehead wrinkled into permanent worry lines.

"Good to see you, Walter. How have you been?"

He ignored the pleasantries and immediately got to the problem, "My sister, Virginia, needs a conservator."

"I think you mean Guardian. Conservator is the name used in some other states, such as California."

"Whatever. She has Alzheimer's, so she needs a Guardian."

I said, "Lots of people have Alzheimer's, and they don't need a Guardian. What happened to make you come here today?"

"Virginia's been sick for a long time. She was doing fine till this year. I had people coming in to clean her condo and take her shopping and to the doctor. A few months ago, she started to go downhill. She can't take care of herself. You know what I mean."

I could see that he was too embarrassed to say that she was incontinent, so I changed the subject to finances, "Have you been paying for her care?"

"I've been using her money from a joint account we have at the bank. Her Social Security and dividends get deposited to the account. I write out the checks for her care, condo fees, taxes — whatever she needs to pay. Now that she's in assisted living her money is going down. Assisted living costs $7,000 a month. Her monthly income is only $2,000 a month. The joint account is down to $15,000. I need to cash in some of her securities to pay for her care. They're in her name so I can't do it."

"From what you are telling me, Virginia does need a Guardian to take care of her everyday living needs and to make her medical decisions. We call that person a *Guardian of the person*. She also needs a *Guardian of her property* to manage her finances. The same person can serve as the Guardian of her person and of her property. Who did you have in mind to serve as Guardian?"

"Me."

I was afraid he was going to say that. In our county, Guardianship matters are handled in the Probate Division of the court. There is only one judge in charge of probate and guardianship matters. I appeared before him many times. I knew he didn't like to appoint an old person to serve as Guardian. What if the Guardian got sick? Walter's sister has Alzheimer's. At his age, Walter might begin to "lose it" as well. That would leave the Court with a Ward and no Guardian. The judge didn't want to be left in the position of scrambling to find a successor Guardian to care for the Ward.

Age discrimination is a legal taboo, so I could not express these concerns to my client. Instead I said, "I don't recall whether Virginia had any children."

"No. She never had children. I'm the only family she has here."

I tried to discourage him. "Becoming a Guardian is no small task. The judge in this county requires Guardians to complete a guardianship course explaining the responsibilities and duties of the Guardian, the rights of the Ward and how to prepare the annual reports required by the Court."

"That's no problem."

"Walter, I'm going to level with you. There is no law in this state that says a family member has priority to be appointed as Guardian. Generally, the judge appoints those closest to the Ward such as spouse, child, parent, sibling, however, the choice is strictly his. If he thinks you are not up to the job, he can appoint a professional Guardian for the job. He could even appoint a not-for-profit corporation as Guardian."

"How could a corporation be a Guardian?"

"There are charitable and religious not-for-profit organizations that employ people to do guardianship work."

The word "religious" set Walter off, "Me and my sister are not religious. I'll fight if any judge tries to shove religion down our throats."

I could see there was no point in trying to convince him that these organizations separated their religious belief from their guardianship duties. "If you have religious concerns, there are people who are engaged in the business of providing guardianship services."

Walter asked, "You mean they charge to be Guardian?"

"Sure they do. Being a Guardian is work. A Guardian needs to visit Virginia on a regular basis to see that she is all right. He needs to see to it that your sister's bills are paid and take care of whatever property Virginia owns."

"I do that already, and I don't take any money."

"As Guardian, you will be entitled to reasonable compensational. How much you get paid is up to the judge. In this county, the going rate is [1]$50 an hour."

Walter was shocked, "Is that what Guardians get paid? No, I don't want no one taking that kind of money from my sister. I'll take care of her like always, and without pay. She needs all of her money to pay for her care. If there is anything left when she dies, I'll inherit it anyway. Look, I'm paying you to get me appointed as Guardian — so you do your job and I'll do mine."

I repressed a sigh, "I'll represent you to the very best of my ability, but you need to understand that I can't control the judge. He is a good judge. He will listen to my argument that you are the one for the job, however, as I explained, the decision is his."

Walter agreed to go forward. "OK. Do the best you can."

"I'll need a retainer of $3,000."

Walter scowled, "What for?"

---

[1] Figures used in this book are approximate values. Amounts are generally higher in large states and lower in states with a small population.

"I need to prepare and file a *Petition for the Appointment of Guardian* and an Application for you to be appointed as her Guardian. There will be a Court hearing to determine whether your sister needs a Guardian which you and I will attend. I need to prepare an order for the judge to sign appointing you as Guardian as well as *Letters of Guardianship* giving you authority to act as Virginia's Guardian."

"Doesn't the judge prepare his own orders?"

I explained, "The attorney prepares the order he wants the judge to sign. If the order is not the way the judge wants to rule, he'll change it. In routine cases like this, orders are standard and the judge just signs them. As you can tell, guardianship is a lot of work. I charge $300 per hour. Once you are appointed as Guardian, you can reimburse yourself from Virginia's guardianship Estate."

"Her guardianship Estate? You mean her money?"

"Yes. When she becomes a Ward, all of her property becomes her guardianship Estate. Once the guardianship is established, you can reimburse yourself for the money you paid to me, and your expenses in establishing the guardianship, such as the check you're going to write to the Clerk of the Court to file your petition to have a Guardian appointed."

"How much is that?"

"$375."

Walter shook his head "That's a lot of money."

I agreed, "That's only the beginning. The judge will send out a *Court Investigator* to verify that Virginia is incapacitated and in need of a Guardian. His fee will be at least $400. It could be significantly higher, depending on how much work is involved in determining whether your sister needs a Guardian.

"All this just to say that she has Alzheimer's and can't take care of herself— which we already know."

I explained, "The judge will not appoint a Guardian for Virginia unless he finds by clear and convincing evidence that she needs one. That means he needs to be really sure she needs a Guardian. The judge will also appoint an attorney to represent your sister so that she will have legal representation at the court hearing."

Walter asked, "What's the point of her having her own lawyer? She doesn't know what's going on."

I explained, "That's to protect people at the hearing so they are not railroaded into a guardianship that they may not need or want. Once we file your application to be appointed Guardian, the judge will issue a Notice giving the time and place of the hearing as well as the matter to be determined at the hearing, namely whether your sister is in need of a Guardian. The Notice will be served on your sister.

"Are they going to have the sheriff go to my sister and hand her this Notice?"

"No, I'll ask the Court to serve the Notice on the attorney appointed by the Court to represent your sister, instead of serving your sister."

"Good. I don't want her to be upset by all this."

I asked, "Does your sister still recognize you?"

"Sure. She looks forward to my visits."

I suggested, "Try to spend as much time as you can with your sister in the next few weeks. It will help your case if you are there when the Court Investigator visits. He will see how attentive you are and how much your sister cares for you. Also, I want you to take the next guardianship class."

Walter asked, "Do I have to pay to take the class?"

"It's a nominal fee, just to cover the cost of the printed material."

"How nominal?"

"Fifty dollars. It important that you take the course before the court hearing. It will give you a better chance of being appointed Guardian, if you go before the Court ready to serve as Guardian as soon as you are appointed."

Walter promised to take the course.

I filed the petition and application with the court. Within the week, I received a copy of the Notice giving the name, address and telephone number of the Court Investigator and of the court appointed attorney. Working in a small community, most of the attorneys know each other, so I was not surprised to see that my friend, Susan Watkins, was appointed by the Court to represent Virginia.

I called Susan. We caught up on family events and then went on to discuss the case. "Walter's sister has Alzheimer's. He's been caring for her for years. Now she's in assisted living and he needs to cash in her securities to pay for her care. I don't know how aware she is of her surroundings. She still recognizes her brother. Did you want him to be present when you speak to her?"

"Yeah, she might be more willing to speak to me if her brother is there."

I called Walter to arrange the meeting. "It is important that you make a good impression with Virginia's attorney. The judge will rely on her opinion more than mine because she represents your sister. Be polite and respectful. Tell her how much you appreciate her serving as Virginia's lawyer. And don't ask how much she is going to charge!"

"You mean I don't have the right to know what she's charging?"

"You'll find out what she charged when she submits her bill to the Court. How much Susan gets paid is up to the judge. He's the one to approve her fee, not you."

Walter worried, "What if she's charging too much?"

"You can raise an objection with the Court. However, I can tell you from past experience that the judge allows the going rate in this county. Whoever is appointed as Guardian will be ordered to pay that amount from the Ward's assets. The Guardian has little to say in the matter. Once you ask to be Guardian, you are submitting yourself to the authority of the Court. You are required to do whatever the judge tells you to do."

Walter didn't say anything, but his expression was one of "What I gotten myself into?"

I received copies of the report submitted to the Court by the Investigator. It was as expected. He agreed that Virginia was in need of a Guardian for her personal needs and a Guardian to manage her property.

Within the month, the judge set the hearing. I prepared Walter for his day in court. I knew Walter had a career in the army, so I prepared him in a way he could relate to — I barked orders at him like a drill sergeant:
"First impressions are important, so come to court in a suit and tie, shoes shined, neat haircut.

— You need to give the judge great respect. Stand straight up when he walks into the room. Do not sit until he tells you to do so.

— I am here to speak for you. Do not speak unless the judge asks you a question. If he does asks you a question, always start your answer with 'Your Honor.'

— Manners count. If you do speak take every opportunity to say 'Please' and 'Thank you.'

— No matter what the judge says, do not correct or contradict him. If he says something wrong, it is my job, to bring the correct fact to his attention — not yours."

"Remember," I continued "he's the guy with the power. If you want to be Guardian, you need to convince him that you are capable of being Guardian, and that you are willing to follow his instructions to the letter."

I guess I used the right approach because Walter appeared on time, clean shaven, suit and tie.

The Court Investigator and Susan, the court appointed attorney, were already there and waiting in the lobby outside Judge Stone's court room when I arrived. I looked at the court roster and saw that we were fifth in line. I prepared Walter for the wait. "These guardianship hearings generally don't last that long. He should take us within the hour."

Walter mumbled something about running the court more efficiently rather than making the public wait. He soon settled down and began to count the people as they went into and then out of the court room.

When it was our turn, Walter stood straight up, and stepped spryly into the court room. He seemed to know, even without my saying, that his age would be a factor if the judge suspected that he might be in poor health or not as sharp as he used to be.

The judge was busy looking at the report submitted by the Court Investigator when we entered the court room. We stood at attention until he looked up and said "Be seated."

Judge Stone turned to Susan and asked, "Do you waive the court appearance of your client?"

Susan said, "Yes, your honor. She has difficulty walking and is generally confused. She doesn't understand what is going on. It would serve no purpose to have her appear before the Court."

The judge said, "Having reviewed the report of the Court Investigator, I am signing an order stating that your client is incapacitated and in need of a Guardian. Ms. Watkins, are there any rights defined by state statute that your client can retain?"

"No, your Honor. She is too ill to do any of them."

""In that case, I find her to be incapacitated and no longer able to:
- (a)   to marry
- (b)   to vote
- (c)   to personally apply for government benefits
- (d)   to have a driver's license
- (e)   to travel
- (f)   to seek or retain employment."

The judge turned his attention to Walter's Application For Appointment As Guardian giving his qualifications. The judge read the Application, and took a hard look at Walter.

I tried to distract the judge's attention from Walter's physical appearance, "Mr. Schnelling has taken the guardianship class. You will see a copy of his completion certificate before you."

Susan chimed in, "Your Honor, the petitioner has been caring for his sister for several years. He has seen to it that she is well cared for. When she was no longer able to care for herself he placed her in Happy Oaks."

The judge asked, "Isn't that an assisted living facility?"

"Yes, Your Honor. In fact, one of the nicest facilities in the county. He visits her every day. It is obvious that there is much affection between them. They have no other relatives in this state. They just have each other. He has been paying her bills with funds from their joint account. That account is running low and he needs to sell her securities to pay for her care."

The judge nodded his head indicating that he would appoint Walter as Guardian. "How much are the securities worth?"

"About $80,000." I answered.

"I'll require a bond in that amount."

Walter felt the judge was questioning his honor. "I'm her brother. I don't need to be bonded."

I winced. Almost as a reflex, I kicked the sole of Walter's shoe under the table.

The judge was not pleased. In a stern voice he said, "My job is to protect your sister's property. Your job is to follow my orders. Pursuant to state statute I require that you be bonded in the amount of $80,000. No Letters shall be issued until you get that bond!"

I answered for Walter, "Yes, your Honor. We will obtain the bond. We'll have it to the Court within the wcck. Thank you, your Honor. Thank you."

I practically bowed as we backed out of the court room.

I arranged for the bond that same day.

Chapter 1a The Rebellious Guardian

Within the week, I received the order appointing Walter as Guardian and his Letters of Guardianship giving him authority to act on behalf of his sister. I called Walter and told him that he had been appointed Guardian and to make an appointment so that I could give him a copy of the order and his Letters. He came in the very next day.

I explained the order to him, "As Guardian of her person you have the right to:
(a) determine her residence
(b) determine who will provide for her personal care
(c) consent to her medical and mental health treatment
(d) make decisions about her social environment or
     other social aspects of her life.
As Guardian of her property, you have the right to do the following on her behalf:
(e) enter into a contract
(f) sue and defend lawsuits
(g) apply for government benefits
(h) manage her property."

Walter wanted to know which of those rights he could use to sell her securities.

I said, "(h) the right to manage her property. That means you can liquidate her securities and use the funds to pay for her care. I got you several certified copies of the Letters to submit when you transact business as her Guardian. You will need to open a separate guardianship bank account to deposit the money from the securities. If there is anything left in her joint account, you need to transfer it into the guardianship account — unless some of that money is yours."

"No. She just put my name on the account so I could pay her bills."

"What were you planning to do with Virginia's condo?

"I wasn't planning on doing anything with it."

I explained, "As Guardian it is your duty to manage her property. That means making it as productive as possible. Leaving it empty costs money. There are condo fees and assessments. There are property taxes. It would be alright to keep it empty if you think there's some hope that she'll return home."

"No. She's never going home."

"Then you need to either rent it out to cover expenses, or sell it and invest the money in securities, or a Certificate of Deposit. Rent or sell, state statute requires you to ask Court permission before you do so."

Walter asked, "You mean we have to go back to court again?"

"I have to go back to court and ask permission. It is not necessary for you to come with me — and after your last run in with the judge, it's best I go alone."

There was a lot more paper work to do. Walter had to file an Initial Guardianship Report with the Court outlining where Virginia would be housed during the year. The report required that he file a summary of Virginia's treatment and rehabilitation needs.

"What treatment. What rehabilitation needs?" asked Walter. "She has Alzheimer's. She not going to get better."

I said, "The best way to complete this report is to attach a letter from her doctor explaining her current treatment and how often he intends to examine her this year. You'll also need to submit an inventory of your sister's property as part of the Initial Guardianship Report. You'll need to have her condo appraised."

Walter wasn't pleased at the thought of paying an appraiser, however by now he figured out there was no point in complaining. He had to do whatever was required by the Court.

I asked, "Did you say you were going to rent or sell Virginia's apartment?"

"I didn't say, but rent, I think."

"OK., I will draft a lease for you to use. It will say that the lease does not become effective until the Court approves the lease agreement. That means you can't let anyone move into the apartment until I get the judge to approve the lease."

"How long is that going to take?" he asked impatiently.

"I can get it approved within the week."

Finally, after a couple of weeks, the condo was leased, all the papers were filed with the court and Walter settled in to doing the same things he had been doing all along — paying Virginia's bills and seeing to her care.

A YEAR LATER

State law requires a Guardian of the property to file an accounting with the Court each year and the Guardian of the person to file an annual report. The annual report tells the Court where the Ward lives, what care she has received during the year and what care is planned for the coming year. Walter, being Guardian of the person and property, needed to file an accounting and a report, so I sent the necessary forms to him. The guardianship course Walter took included a lesson on how to complete these reports. Still I thought it best to include a letter explaining the forms to refresh his memory.

Walter was on the phone as soon as the mail came in. Apparently he had forgotten all about the guardianship course, "More paper? And what? I have to pay you to send me these forms and file this, this . . . junk with the court? Do you know how much it cost to get me appointed Guardian? Over $6,000 that's how much. Do you know the Clerk charged me $100 just to audit the inventory I sent in? What was there to audit? I attached the appraisal to the inventory — which I had to pay $1,000 for. And for what? Just to cash in a few stocks so I can take care of my sister?"

"I agree. There should be a simplified guardianship procedure for cases such as yours. Still, your sister brought all this on herself. Remember when you both came into my office for your Wills? We discussed a Power of Attorney at that time. Virginia wanted a Will, and nothing more. If she had given you a Power of Attorney while she was alert and able to sign her name, you could have sold her stocks, rented out her condo — yes, even sold her condo, all on your own signature as her Agent."

Actually, I was being kind. Walter was just as much, if not more, at fault than Virginia. Alzheimer's is a slow progressive disease. Virginia probably was not aware that her mind was fading. But Walter knew. He should have thought ahead and made plans for the day when Virginia would not be able to manage her finances.

I saw no point in scolding Walter. Instead, I tried to get him to think of his own well being. "What happened to your sister could happen to you. You should be thinking about who will care for you in case you get sick. You said you had two cousins who live in New York. Do you keep in touch with them?"

"Sure. They're very nice."

"You should be thinking about giving one of them a Power of Attorney in case you take sick."

"Me? No. I'm fine. It's just this guardianship stuff makes me crazy."

AND ANOTHER YEAR LATER

I sent out the annual accounting form and the annual guardianship report to Walter. I expected that having gone through the process last year, he would just do it without complaining. I was wrong. He was upset and made an appointment for an office visit.

"Do you know how much it cost last year just to report to the Court. Over $1,000 that's how much. Do you know the Clerk charged me $150 just to audit the accounting? And I had to get a doctor to go out and examine Virginia and file his report with the Plan. That cost me another $400. What's to examine? She has Alzheimer's. That isn't going to change this year. Why should I get him out again to have him write the same thing he wrote last year?"

My attorney fees did not escape his wrath, "And what? I have to pay you just to mail me the same form you sent last year? Why do I need a lawyer anyway? I know how to file these forms by myself. You made me take that guardianship class. I sat there for hours. I learned how to fill out these forms. And I know the law. The law says everyone has the right to represent himself. I want to represent myself. I'll take care of the filing myself!"

"Walter, if you look at the forms you'll see that the Guardian's lawyer has to sign the reports. If you try to send in the forms without my signature, the Clerk will just bounce it back to you. No. The only one who can release me from this case is the judge."

"You mean I can't even fire you!"

"Yes, you can fire me, but you need to get another lawyer to represent you as Guardian, and we will all need to go to court and have the judge approve the change of lawyers."

"That can't be true. I saw this guy on TV who shot a man outside of a synagogue. The judge let him represent himself in his trial for murder, even though the guy was old, could barely speak English, and if you ask me, a little bit senile. If he could represent himself for murder, why can't I represent myself in this guardianship?"

"My job is to represent you as Guardian. I'm not representing you personally. "

"What, are you playing word games with me ? I AM the Guardian?"

"No. I'm being paid with Virginia's money to represent her Guardian, who just happens to be you. You're not paying me with your money. I am not representing you as Walter, I'm representing you as Guardian."

Walter had that same expression that I saw when he found out that he had no control over what Susan was going to charge as Virginia's court appointed attorney. He had no more control over his (and Virginia's) fate than a fly caught in a spider's web — only he was caught in the legal web called guardianship.

I was sympathetic to Walter's plight. I could understand his feeling of helplessness. I tried to assure him that the legal system did allow for some flexibility in those cases that require minimal accounting, "State statute allows a Guardian to submit his own annual accounting in special cases where all of the Ward's money is kept in one bank and the money is just kept there without any being spent to take care of the Ward during the year."

I could see from the glint in Walter's eye that even mentioning a lawyerless accounting was a mistake. He said, "If they allow it in some cases, they can allow it in mine."

"No Walter. The law is limited to those cases where no money is being spent from the guardianship account, and no other funds are coming into the account. You spend a lot of Virginia's money each year for her care, and you have to account to the Court for the income you get from the rental of her condo."

"I'm not saying that I don't want to give an accounting, I'm just saying that I don't need to pay you to sign a piece of paper. I'll explain to the judge that I'm her brother. Even if I weren't, he made me get a bond that protects her money. I want you to ask the judge to let me take care of this guardianship by myself."

"No. Walter, that would be a big mistake. The judge won't let you turn in the reports without me. Sure I can draft a petition and ask for permission for you to serve without a lawyer — but he will certainly deny the request. It will be a total waste of Virginia's money to pay me to draft the petition and then accompany you to court to argue a sure-to-lose cause."

I guess Walter thought that I was just trying to protect my income as attorney for the Guardian, because he discounted my advice and said, "We can at least ask the judge to let me serve without a lawyer. I'll talk to him. I'll explain how I took the courses. I'll promise him that I will turn in all reports exactly on time."

"That isn't going to work. He already knows that you took the course. The law requires that you turn in the reports on time, so why should he be swayed by your promise that you're going to do what you're supposed to do anyway? No. Walter. This is a bad idea."

Walter was a take charge kind of guy all of his life. Having to buckle to this legal system was too much for him to take lying down. Fighting the system at least gave him some feeling of control. He refused to be denied his day in court. "We're at least going to try," he insisted.

Walter was in good spirits as we waited for our turn to go before the judge. Just the thought that he might have some degree of autonomy was worth the try — even if it meant he had to pay legal fees from the guardianship account to argue the point in court.

I was not in such good spirits. In fact, my stomach was in knots bracing for the blast that was sure to come from the judge once he read the petition.

And blast he did. "Sir, let me make this clear to you. I don't need you. I can replace you with a professional Guardian in a second. I do need your lawyer. It's your lawyer who knows all of the guardianship rules. Your lawyer is an officer of this Court. As officer of this Court it's her job it is to see to it that all of the guardianship rules are obeyed. It's her job to work with me to see that this guardianship is properly administered. Petition denied!"

And he banged his gavel for emphasis.

SIX MONTHS LATER

After the court fiasco, Walter completed the required reports. I signed them and filed them with the court. I did not expect to hear from him until next year, so I was surprised to see that Walter made an appointment for an office visit.

As he came into the room he said, "Virginia died."

"I'm sorry to hear that. Are you OK.?"

"Yeah. Living with Alzheimer's is worse than dying. She couldn't speak, she couldn't walk. She stopped eating. It's better she died."

"Yes, but it's still hard." I said.

With rounded shoulders, he nodded in agreement.

I thought it would help to get Walter busy closing out the guardianship, "There are forms you will need to complete to terminate the guardianship."

"Of course. What else is new?"

I gave him the forms, "You need to file a final report, and a Petition For Discharge as Guardian."

"I'll fill them out and mail that back to you."

"Before you leave, we need to discuss the probate of Virginia's Estate. As I recall, Virginia had a Will that left everything to you."

"Yes, we only had each other."

I explained what we would need to do in order to transfer Virginia's funds to Walter, "The guardianship judge is also in charge of probate, so he can appoint you as Personal Representative of Virginia's Estate. You, as Guardian, will transfer her property to you as Personal Representative. Then you, as Personal Representative will transfer Virginia's property to you as her sole beneficiary."

"Sounds complicated." Walter said.

"It's not. It's just a lot of paper work. Because you are sole beneficiary, I can ask the judge for a Summary Administration — that's a simplified probate proceeding. I should have title to the condo transferred to you within a couple of months. The cost of the probate, start to finish, should be less than a thousand dollars. "

"That's nothing compared to what I spent for guardianship. Too bad they don't have a simplified guardianship."

I agreed with him, "Yes. Even with a complicated probate, there's an end in sight. Once the money is distributed, it's over. Not so with guardianship. As you know from personal experience, guardianship goes on year after year, after year, until the Ward is restored to health or dies."

How Virginia Could Have
Avoided Guardianship

As explained in the Introduction of this book, Part II of this book rewrites each of the seven stories of Part I to show how guardianship could have been avoided in each case. I could have organized this book by telling the story and following it up with an explanation of how to avoid guardianship. I didn't go that route for two reasons:

CONTINUITY

Each story in Part I of the book shows a different aspect of the guardianship procedure. By reading these stories in sequence, you (the reader) will get an overall view of the guardianship procedure.

TO HOLD YOUR INTEREST

Explaining how to avoid guardianship involves an explanation of the Power of Attorney, the Health Care Directive, the Trust, the Preneed Guardian, etc. These are fairly sophisticated legal concepts. My goal was to explain these guardianship-avoiding tools in an interesting, easy to understand, manner. Still, these topics are somewhat technical, and I didn't want to interrupt the flow of the short story section of this book. However, if you have a situation similar to this story, namely an elderly, single person being cared for by a close family member, and you want to know how to avoid guardianship — right now, you can turn to page 172.

Chapter 1 Rewrite
Avoiding Guardianship For The Elderly

Once you complete that section, come back to page 27. The Mollie story is a page turner.

The Mentally Ill Ward 2

Mollie was pushing a shopping cart down the street. She was wearing a heavy jacket, which was strange considering it was 80^0 in the shade. She bumped her cart into an elderly man who happened to be walking on the street. It wasn't that she didn't see him. It was the only way she could express her anger — at him, society and the world in general. The man croaked angrily at her, "What's the matter with you? Are you crazy?"

She continued down the street trying to hit as many people as possible. A patrol car happened by. The two officers observed a few minutes and then came out to speak to her.

"Off your meds, Mollie?"

If she was angry before, asking about her meds unleashed all of the demons that plagued her.

"Now Mollie, I haven't heard that kind of talk since I arrested a drunk sailor over at the bar. Come on, let's take you home."

There was no way to settle her down. She screamed, kicked, scratched and tried to bite the officers. Finally, they handcuffed her and drove her off to jail.

The police chief groaned, "Mollie, again? I thought her son arranged for a housekeeper to stay with her. Go over to her house and see what's going on."

A disheveled man opened the door to Mollie's house. He looked, and smelled, hung over.

One of the officers said, "I thought Mollie Goran lived here."

"She sold the house to me."

The other officer asked, "When did she do that?"

"A few months ago."

The officers glanced into the doorway and noticed that the house looked much the same as when Mollie lived there.

"Didn't she take her furniture?"

"No, she sold it with the house. I can show you the deed. I'll go get it."

The officers looked at each other with that 'something doesn't smell right' look.

The man came back with the deed. "See, all proper signed and recorded. Look."

The deed was one of those preprinted quit-claim deeds that could be purchased from any office supply store.

The officer asked, "Did you use a lawyer to buy the house?"

"We got a notary to help us sign the deed and get it recorded. I didn't do anything wrong. Mollie and I are friends. She needed the money. I needed a place to live, so we made a deal."

"How much did you pay for the house?"

"I'm gonna pay her $100,000. I already paid $10,000 and I'm gonna give her another $500 a month until it's all paid."

"Did you give her a mortgage?"

"I told you. We're friends. She trusts me 'n I trust her."

"Have you paid her anything since closing?"

"I couldn't find her. I have the money. All she has to do is come by. I'll pay her."

The officers left. Although they suspected that the man had conned Mollie out of her home, there wasn't much they could do without Mollie filing a complaint — and she was in no condition to do that. The best they could do was to keep her in jail until they could release her to the custody of her son.

The police captain called Paul at his office in Washington, D.C. and told him that they had his mother in jail. Paul had an important job with the government. Even though he was working on a pressing project, he dropped everything a nd took the next flight in.

His meeting with his mother was painful — as always. He tried not to look at her matted hair or dirty clothing. He tried not to notice the faint scent of garbage. He tried not to cry.

"Mom. I brought you your medicine. You need to take it."

She looked at him as if he were a monster. "No. No. NO! I know what you're doing. You're trying to KILL ME!"

He left her in the cell, and went out to talk to the police captain, "This is the worst I've seen her in a long time. She doesn't seem to know me. We'll need to put her in the hospital until we can get her back on medication."

"OK. I'll call Mercy Hospital. Their psychiatric unit should have her records. She's been there before. I'll have a couple of my officers take her there."

Paul shook his head in disbelief, "I don't understand. Things were going so well. She seemed to like the housekeeper I hired. I don't know what went wrong."

The captain told him about the officer's investigation.

Paul was furious. "She didn't know what she was doing. That house is worth $200,000. He took advantage of her. I'll bet he never even gave her the $10,000. Did she have any money on her when you picked her up?"

"No. Nothing."

"Can't you arrest him?"

"I could put him away if he stole money — even ten dollars — if he robbed her at gun point. Proving that he scammed her out of her home is something else. People make bad judgments in life all the time. No Court ever determined that she didn't have the ability to manage her money, so she was free to sell her home — even for half price. The buyer will say that he just made a good bargain, and that is not against the law. No. Stealing her house is forging her signature on the deed, or forcing her to sign the deed against her will."

Paul was frustrated. "Isn't conning an insane person out of her home a crime?"

"Sure, if he knew she was insane. When she's taking her medicine, you wouldn't know it. And did he actually con her into thinking her home was worth only $100,000? Maybe she wanted to sell her home and that's the price she asked for it."

"Can't you at least bring him in for questioning?"

"We need some reason to believe that a crime was committed before we can do that. We checked out his police record to see if he had any convictions for fraud. All we found was a misdemeanor arrest when he was drunk. We did get a copy of the deed from the court house. Here it is."

Paul looked at the deed and agreed that it was his mother's signature.

The captain explained, "It is hard to prove a white collar crime. We need the victim to press charges and Mollie can't do that. Even if she were well enough to say he swindled her, we'd have to prove the charges *beyond a reasonable doubt*. Hard to do if only the two of them were present when she agreed to the sale. A good defense lawyer could easily show that your mother has trouble telling fact from fiction. Unless the buyer had a long criminal history of embezzlement or fraud, I doubt whether the prosecutor will agree to even investigate. Your better bet is to get a guardianship and then sue the buyer in civil court. There you just have to prove a *preponderance of the evidence*. All the judge has to find is that it is more likely than not that Mollie did not know what she was doing when she signed the deed. Once he makes that finding, he can rescind the deed and Mollie will have her home back."

"How do I get a guardianship?"

The captain advised, "It's pretty complicated. Get a lawyer who is experienced in guardianship."

Which is how I came to meet Paul.

He was tall, thin and dressed sort of nouveau riche casual — open collared shirt, expensive loafers, the latest designer wristwatch. He had an intense, almost intimidating, presence. He stood there stiffly. I asked him to be seated and he sat down, stiffly. I thought to myself that this fellow's generation is more at ease with computers than with people.

After hearing his story, I said, "Yes, your mother certainly does need a Guardian. However, I am an Elder Law attorney. I do probate, guardianship, estate planning. I don't do litigation. You would probably do better to employ a large firm with attorneys who do guardianship and attorneys who do litigation."

"No. I don't like dealing with large law firms — I do that all day at work. Don't you know a lawyer who could handle the lawsuit?"

I smiled and said, "There's a law firm in this building with a trial lawyer who's tenacious as a bull dog. The firm keeps him in a room at the end of the hall and throws him red meat once a week."

He gave me a blank stare.

I explained, "That's a lawyer joke."

I thought, 'OK. Best just to stick to the business at hand.'

I suggested, "You have time to decide who to employ to fight the case. Right now we need to get a Guardian appointed for your mother. Once the Guardian is appointed he can ask the judge for permission to file the lawsuit on behalf of your mother. In a case like this, it's best to have a relative who lives close by to serve as Guardian. Does your mother have any relative who lives here in New York ?"

"No. My father used to live here with my mother. He gave her their home as part of their divorce settlement. He doesn't want to have any contact with her, still he wants to be sure that she's all right. He gives me money each month for her care. I use the money to pay for her housekeeper and the upkeep of the house. I give her whatever is left for as pocket money."

This verified my initial observation that money was not his problem. His problem was trying to take care of his mother. I asked, "Does your mother have anything other than the house?"

"No. She's on Social Security disability. That's barely enough to support her. That's why my father subsidizes her, even though he's not legally obligated to do so. He considers the money he gives to me as a gift. "

Generally, I ask for a retainer of $3,000, however I could see this was going to be a difficult case on many levels, "I'll need $5,000 as a retainer, plus you will need to pay the court filing fees and other costs associated with setting up the guardianship, such as paying the Court Investigator to verify that your mother is incapacitated. If the lawsuit goes well, you can use the money from the sale of the house to reimburse yourself. If not, you — or your father, will be out that money. "

We went over all of the things he needed to do to become Guardian. He was impatient with all of the paper work, and downright annoyed at the educational requirement. "I can only take so much time away from my work. I have an MBA from Georgetown University. Can't I take a correspondence course or a test?"

"Taking the course is part of your duty as a Guardian. My telling the judge that you can't take time off from your job to take the course will not sit well. He isn't going to be too thrilled that you live in another state as it is. Remember the choice of Guardian is his. If we push this education thing, he may decide to appoint a local professional Guardian to care for your mother. Look, you don't to take the course until you are appointed Guardian. You'll probably need to be here anyway to visit your mother or to work on the lawsuit."

That seemed to satisfy him, so we completed the paper work, and I filed the petition with the court.

The following week I got a call from Richard, one of my fellow graduates from law school. He had been appointed by the court to represent Mollie at the guardianship hearing. He asked, "How long has she been this sick?"

"I don't know. From what I can see from the records, her mental illness goes back to Paul's birth. There wasn't any problem before that — or if there was a problem, there's no record of it. After the birth, she seemed to go into a postpartum depression. Paul's father said that the depression was so severe that he feared Mollie might hurt their baby, so he had her hospitalized and had his mother take care of Paul. After that, it was in and out of treatment facilities."

Richard had the file in front of him, "Yeah, this medical record is six inches thick. I see all kinds of diagnoses from obsessive compulsive to paranoia to schizophrenia."

I wondered, "Did you get a chance to meet her?"

"I did. She comes across as mostly rational. She doesn't want a guardianship. She says that she has been mis-diagnosed, or as she calls it over-diagnosed. She said she knew what she was doing when she sold the house. She didn't want to be tied down to one place. The monthly income would give her the freedom to stay whereever she wishes."

I answered sarcastically, "Apparently, where she wishes to live is on the street, and off her medication, pushing shopping carts into people — cause that's how the police found her. She was getting money from Paul each month. Why did she think she needed to sell the house to get more money?"

Richard said, "She told me that she doesn't want to be told where to live. And she doesn't want Paul giving her money. She wants her own money. She says he treats her like a child. She absolutely doesn't want him to be her Guardian. She wants me to fight this whole thing."

I could hear the stress in Richard's voice. I understood his dilemma. It was the unresolved problem of what to do with those who are mentally ill. Do you restrict their activities, or do you give them the freedom to wander the streets, so long as they do not hurt themselves or others? Society has opted for the latter. Yet how can living on the streets in all kinds of weather, not bathing, searching garbage for discarded food, not be harmful to these victims of mental illness?

Richard had conflicting legal duties. He was charged with the vigorous representation of his client. That meant fighting the guardianship as hard as he could vs. representing the best interests of his client. But was it in his client's best interest to go back to the street? Maybe never collect the money for the house?

I thought of a compromise, "It sounds to me like what Mollie is really upset about is the high-handed manner in which Paul treats her. She wants to be treated like the mother, not the child. We could present the problem to her psychologist and ask him to work with Mollie and Paul to establish better lines of communication. If that is successful, you and I can meet with our clients and work out a limited guardianship."

"Yeah. Mollie could keep her right to vote, travel, and most importantly, determine where she gets to live."

"I have no problem with the right to travel, provided she lets Paul know where she's going and when she gets back. She can retain the right to determine her residence, again provided she lets Paul know when and where she intends to move. As for the money, we could explain to her that once the lawsuit is settled, Paul could invest the money and have the income sent directly to her each month — only on condition that she keeps taking her medicine. Deal's off any time she stops taking it. That might keep her motivated to stay on her medication."

Richard liked the idea of a negotiation rather than a court battle over whether Mollie was in need of a Guardian. "Sounds like a plan. I'll ask the judge for a continuance of the hearing to give us time to work out the details. I hope this works, if not I'll see you in court."

I was very pleased with myself for having thought of a way to avoid a hearing where the capacity of the Ward to manage her own affairs was being contested. I had only one of those in my career and it was not fun.

I could hardly wait to tell Paul the good news. However, his response was a bucket of cold water tossed in my face. "You're making it sound like all this is my fault! It's easy to say that the problem is the way I've been treating her. I've seen three year olds who act better than she does. All she does is throw temper tantrums. That's why I treat her like a child. I told you that she doesn't have any family. That's not true. She has a sister and nieces and nephews. They all turned their backs on her. I'm the only one left. You don't know what I've been putting up with all these years. Maybe I should turn my back on her too and just go on with my life. Let her become a street person. That's what she really wants. Why should I care?"

"Paul, I couldn't for one second imagine how hard it's been for you. No one would fault you for walking away. That's what happens to so many of the families of those who are mentally ill — they just get tired of trying. That's why you can go to any big city and see deranged people wandering the streets. I understand that this whole thing is a lot to ask of you. The guardianship course, the reports to the court, the lawsuit. It can go on for years. In the end, your mother may not be one bit better off than she is today."

He wasn't responding, so I suggested he choose a professional Guardian to serve in his place.

I told him, "I surely will not think less of you if you decided to let a professional Guardian take over. You can select a Guardian who you think is best suited to work with your mother. I can arrange to have you interview a Guardians who is experienced in caring for those who are mentally ill. Think it over and let me know."

He called the next day with directions for me to arrange the counseling session. No pleasantries, no apology, no discussion, just orders to do it. I was beginning to understand how Mollie felt.

Within a few weeks I received a call from Richard. "I don't know if these counseling sessions are doing much good. Let's set up a meeting to try to work out the details of the guardianship, anyway. Mollie is taking her medicine. She was stable enough to transfer from Mercy Hospital to a group home. We can meet there."

You could see the resemblance between Mollie and Paul. They had the same green eyes. She was almost as tall as her son and just as thin. Her red hair, though graying, was still wavy. She took an instant liking to me. I tried to explain that I represented Paul, still she insisted on sitting next to me and talking to me instead of her lawyer. She wanted to confide in me. "It's nice here. But I can't wait to get out. They tell me when to eat, when to get up. They want me to talk when I don't feel like talking."

Richard began to explain that it was necessary to have Paul appointed as Guardian to get her house back. That only upset Mollie. She wanted me to understand why she had to leave the house, however all that came out was a discussion of colors. "I couldn't stay in that house. Yellow always causes trouble," she said earnestly. "I can manage with blue. I can't handle yellow."

I offered the obvious solution, "Paul could paint the house blue."

She looked at me with one of those, 'You dear thing. You don't have a clue about what I'm saying.' She went on to explain that yellow is not paint. Yellow is a presence. Something of substance. Something you can feel and taste and smell. "Yellow just wouldn't stay in one room. It smelled up the whole house. I could feel it everywhere. I couldn't get it to leave. Yellow is horrible. It's evil — very, very evil."

Richard, Paul and I looked at each other. There was no point in continuing the discussion. We said our good-byes and went to a local restaurant to work out the details of the guardianship over a cup of coffee. We agreed that Mollie would remain in the group home with 24 hour supervision until her psychiatrist determined she was well enough to move to supported housing, i.e., independent living, with the assistance of with a case manager. After that she could choose her place of resi-dence, provided she let Paul know in advance when and where she intended to move. Initially, Paul would have full guardianship, i.e., Guardian of her person and of her property.

Richard wanted to continue to represent Mollie after Paul was appointed as Guardian, so that as Mollie's lawyer he could petition the court for a less restrictive guardianship once the lawsuit was over and she was stable enough to live on her own.

Generally, the attorney asks to be discharged as the Ward's attorney as soon as the Guardian is appointed. I thought to myself that having Richard continue to represent Mollie was going to be one expensive guardianship.

I could see the need for Mollie's continued representation, still I was concerned about the cost. In an effort to keep Richard's fees to a minimum, I said, "I have no problem with you continuing as Mollie's lawyer after Paul is appointed, however she has no asset other than the house. If Paul doesn't win the lawsuit, there will be no funds available to pay you. The judge will expect you to continue working Pro Bono."

Richard was an experienced Elder Law attorney, so he knew that what I was saying was true. Judges expect lawyers to donate time in service to the poor — especially if that poor person is the Ward whose money runs out during the course of the guardianship.

Richard didn't comment, yet I knew he got the message namely: don't run up a lot of hours. It could happen you are never paid.

The capacity hearing went smoothly. Richard waived Mollie's appearance, saying she was not well enough to comprehend the nature of the hearing. The report of the Court Investigator and the six inch medical file documenting her illness was enough for the judge. He vdeclared her to be in need of a Guardian.

I gave the judge a copy of the police report of the investigation of the ownership of Mollie's home, the quit-claim deed, and an appraisal of Mollie's home showing it had a market value of $225,000.

The judge appointed Paul as his mother's Guardian with full authority to sue the buyer on behalf of Mollie.

Chapter 2a The Helpless Guardian

I recalled the advice given by my law school professor "10% of your clients cause 90% of your problems. Get rid of that 10% and you'll have a great practice."

I thought of those sage words every time I had to deal with Paul. The problem was that I could not just resign from the case without having another lawyer take my place. I had a reputation of being most attentive to the needs of my clients. I knew the other Elder Law lawyers in our small community would be reluctant to take on a client who I was trying to dump. So, I continued.

"Paul, this is the third message I've left on your answering machine. I need to speak to you **NOW.**"

Two days later he returned my call. No apology. Just what did I want?

"I explained before you were appointed as Guardian that there are certain things you need to do. I sent you the inventory form and the form for the Initial Guardianship Report weeks ago. You need to complete these forms so that I can file them with the court."

"I can complete the inventory. That's easy. She doesn't have anything except her monthly income from Social Security. I can't complete the Report because the form asks where she's going to live during the year. I don't have any idea where that will be. It depends on whether she takes her medicine, and how stable she is. For all I know she may end up back on the street."

"Not a good answer, Paul. What ever you turn in must be approved by the Court."

Trying to contain my irritation, I said, "Telling the Court that she could end up on the street is a great way for you to be discharged as her Guardian. Just say where she is now, and where you expect she will be housed once she's discharged from the group home. Have her psychologist write a letter recommending supported housing once she is discharged from the group home and attach it to the Initial Guardianship Report."

"OK., I'll have it to you next week."

"Don't hang up. We still need to arrange for you to take the guardianship class."

"I've already taken too much time away from work. I won't be able to return for at least a month."

"What about the litigation? Did you employ someone for the job?"

I could hear the frustration his voice, "No one wants to take the case on contingency. They all want a big retainer."

I finally figured out was going on. It was no wonder Paul was reluctant to complete his guardianship requirements. He was having second thoughts about the whole thing. The only reason he wanted the guardianship was to get the house back. He thought he could get a lawyer to take the case for a percentage of the recovery, and no money out of pocket. The fact that experienced trial lawyers wanted an hourly rate and money up front made Paul think there was a good chance he might lose the case — as well as all the money he invested in pursuing the guardianship.

I explained to Paul, "Most lawyers work on contingency for personal injury cases because there are insurance funds available and they expect to get a piece of the insurance pie. In this case, there is a house and a victim who will either be unable to testify, or who will testify that she sold the house for the agreed price. Whoever takes the case won't know how strong a case you have until he does some discovery. If the lawyer finds that the buyer knew that your mother was mentally ill, or that he never did give her any money, the lawyer will be confident that he can win. However, he won't know that until he takes the buyer's deposition. That's why the lawyer wants you to pay a retainer up front, so that the risk is on you. You, or your father, need to decide whether to take that financial risk. I suggest you make the decision the same way you make a business decision, namely risk vs. reward. How much of a financial risk do you need to take? How much of a profit can you expect? Then you need to decide whether the potential reward is worth the risk."

He said he would talk it over with his father and get back to me. He didn't. Instead I got a call from the lawyer Paul employed to sue the buyer. The lawyer asked for the court file and Mollie's medical records. I made them available to him, and suggested he call Richard to see if he could assist in any way. In return, I asked him to lean on Paul to do all of the things he needed to do to establish the guardianship, "It's not going to look good for your case if Paul is terminated as Guardian for not complying with the rules of the Court."

The strategy worked. Within the month Paul completed the guardianship course and submitted the Initial Guardianship Report. I would not need to interface with Paul until the next year when Annual Guardianship Report was due.

THE FOLLOWING YEAR

"You lost your mother?" I could hardly contain my anger.

"I didn't *lose* her. I just don't know where she is. I couldn't keep her confined forever. She went from the group home to supported housing. After a few weeks she called saying she wanted to move. I arranged for her to stay in a hotel. I sent her a cell phone so she could keep in touch with me. She seemed to like the hotel best of all — no household responsibilities, no one to tell her what to do. In a couple of months, she wanted to move again. She told me that people were watching her. I could tell she wasn't taking her pills again. But what can I do? I can't force her into treatment unless I can show she is a danger to herself or others — so I told her to find another hotel and let me know where she was. That was a few weeks ago. I haven't heard from her. I don't know if her cell phone is not working, or she just doesn't want to answer it."

I could hear the helplessness in his voice. He was upset that he didn't know where his mother was. He seemed to be at a loss to know what to do.

"Let's start looking for her" I suggested, "I'll check the local hospitals to see if she's been admitted anywhere. You call the police captain and ask whether he has her in jail. If not, have him check other precincts to see if she's been picked up in another county. Maybe you can check with the telephone company and see if they have a tracking devise on the phone. We'll put off the Annual Guardianship Report identifying her residence until we can find her. You can still complete the annual accounting."

"There's no money left."

"No money?? What happened to the house?"

"My trial lawyer insisted we settle the case. I don't know why they call them trial lawyers," he said sarcastically, "About the last thing a trial lawyer wants to do is go to trial. He convinced me that without testimony from my mother, the jury probably would not think that a crime had been committed. So I settled. I had to return the $10,000 to that scam artist — which he probably never paid to my mother in the first place. I had to pay his lawyer $12,000 before he would agree to settle the case. And that drunken con man left the house in a mess. The best I could get for it was $185,000, with me paying all of the closing costs. I paid the trial lawyer. I even had to pay Richard to go to court to get the judge to approve the settlement. I reimbursed myself for all the money I put out to set up the guardianship — the filing fees, the Court Investigator, Richard's fees to represent my mother. I paid my Guardian fees and I reimbursed myself for the money I paid you and all the money I spent flying back and forth this past year. Keeping my mother in the group home was very expensive, so was the hotel she stayed in. I can account for every dime."

"OK. You may need to employ an accountant to assist with completing the accounting forms I sent to you. You will need to include all of the receipts in the annual accounting."

"No. I don't need an accountant. They taught all that to me when I took the guardianship course — and besides, I have an accounting background."

Paul didn't call again. I did get a call from Richard. "Mollie wants to have her legal rights restored."

"Really? Where did you find her?"

"I didn't actually speak to her. Paul's been in touch with her. He tells me he got her to take her medicine in exchange for ending the guardianship and restoring all of her legal rights."

I suspected it was really Paul who wanted to terminate the guardianship. Mollie was too sick to attend the court hearing. I doubted whether she even knew she that her son was appointed as her Guardian. I didn't fault Paul. What good is a guardianship when you are dealing with someone who has a mental illness? Sure the judge can say that Paul is in charge of where his mother lives. But how can the Court enforce Paul's decision? If Mollie walks away, what is the judge going to do? Put her in jail? To Mollie, being in a jail is better than being in the psychiatric Ward of a hospital, or in a group home. At least in jail, no one pestered her to take her medicine.

You may be thinking that at least they got Mollie's house back. However, from Paul's viewpoint the net result was that it made a bunch of lawyer —not Mollie, just that much richer. Paul decided there was little the legal system had to offer his mother. He didn't need a judge to tell him to take care of his mother. He had been doing that all along and that's what he would continue to do. The sooner he could disengage himself as Guardian, the better.

Richard and I worked together to take the necessary steps to terminate the guardianship. He filed a *Petition to Terminate Guardianship* asking the Court to restore all of Mollie's rights and to discharge Paul as Guardian.

Richard and Paul accompanied Mollie to the court house. She looked better than when I saw her last. She remembered me, and as before, wanted to sit beside me and chat.

When it came to our time before the judge, I let Richard take the lead to convince the judge that Mollie was well enough to care for herself and her property. He had the doctor's reports saying that she was a very intelligent person and could take care of herself — provided she continued to take her medication. The judge turned to Mollie, and in a gentle voice said, "From what I see, you're fine so long as you take your anti-psychotic. . ."

The word "psychotic" set Mollie off. She shouted, "I'm not crazy! Those doctors don't know what they're talking about. They're all wrong. Don't believe anything they say. All they want to do is talk and push pills."

"You need to continue taking your medicine," the judge said sternly, "If not, I will have you declared to be incapacitated once again. Petition granted."

Richard and I hurried Mollie out of the court room. We said our good-byes in the hallway and Mollie went off arm in arm with her son.

Richard and I were both relieved that it was all over. He said, "I thought sure the judge was going to deny the petition. He had to have seen that she was still disturbed."

"Yes, yet he also knew that she was without money, and that her son was still going to be there to care for her. What point would it have been to keep her in the court system?"

"Yes, I guess that's exactly what he was thinking."

How Mollie Could Have
Avoided Guardianship

Some readers may want to learn how to avoid guardianship for those who are mentally ill, before going on to read the next Chapter. If you wish to read:

Chapter 2 Rewrite

Avoiding Guardianship For Those Who Are Mentally Ill

before continuing on with the short story section, you can skip to the page 184. However, you first need to read the Rewrite of Chapter 1. It is much like Chapter 1 of this first section of the book because it explains basic terminology. Specifically, the Durable Power of Attorney and the Health Care Directive are basic to the avoidance of guardianship. Pages 172 through 183 explain these two important documents.

It is important to read Chapter 1 Rewrite before you read any of the subsequent Rewrite Chapters.

The Accident Victim 3

It is the practice in our county to rotate judges. Every five years, the chief judge decides which judge will preside over the probate division — which includes guardianship. Judge Stone had been our probate judge for five years. He was consistently rated as one of the best judges in the county. He respected the lawyers that came before his Court, and they respected him. He didn't play favorites. He ruled according to the law. If it was a close call, he listened carefully to both sides. Probably 90% of the time we could predict his ruling. For a lawyer, predictability is most important. As we saw in the last two chapters, I could tell my clients with confidence how the judge would rule.

Yet nothing in life is static. If you are going through good times, you can bet it wouldn't last forever. Of course, if you're going through bad times, there is the consolation that this too shall pass. But when?

Rumor was rampant in our Elder Law community that Judge Wecco was going to replace Judge Stone. My friend, Susan, called me with the news. "It's official. Judge *Wacko* is going to replace Judge Stone."

"No!"

"Yes. Stone is going to the Juvenile Division. Wecco is coming here from Family Court. Everyone there hates him. Plaintiff's lawyers, defendant's lawyers, it makes no difference. He pisses them all off. "

"Well at least he doesn't play favorites."

Susan was not to be appeased, "I'd rather have a crooked judge. At least you know where he's coming from. With this guy there's no telling how he's going to rule."

I appeared before Judge Wecco within the first month of his appointment. It was just my luck to bring one of my toughest cases before him in our first encounter.

It all started simply enough with a visit from Edeeshia Hooper. She came into my office. No, she made an *entrance* into my office. She had the grace and poise of a model. And she looked like one. Tall, a bit on the thin side. Perfect posture. Perfect features. Perfect makeup. Perfect everything. She was dark skinned, yet it was hard to tell whether she was African American, Indian, Polynesian, or some combination of these. Her speech did not give away her heritage. She spoke perfect English — with a hint of an English accent.

I met Edeeshia a few months earlier at one of those high society functions. The party was organized to raise money for a local charity. Large round tables were set up for dinner. She and her husband happened to sit at my table. Dinner was noisy with waiters coming and going, people talking and a band playing. We didn't get much of a chance to talk. Apparently she remembered me and the fact that I was a lawyer, because here she was.

"My husband, Ben, was in a car accident last month."

"I'm sorry to hear that," I said.

Edeeshia continued, "No one knows how it happened. He was on his way home from work when his car rolled over an embankment. Ben has high blood pressure. Doctors don't know if he had a stroke and that's what caused him to lose control of the car, or whether he fell asleep at the wheel and hit his head. I guess it doesn't make any difference because he's in a coma. No one knows when, or even if, he'll ever wake up. There is nothing more they can do for him in the hospital. They want me to transfer him from the hospital to a nursing home. The problem is that the nursing home wants me to pay for the first two months before they will admit him."

I was puzzled. Edeeshia was wearing a designer suit. It appeared to me to be an original — not one of those knock-offs of a big name that you can buy in a department store. Her wedding ring alone had to be worth thousands of dollars.

I guess she noticed my queried look because she went on to explain, "I don't have any money of my own. I mean I have a credit card that Ben pays every month. I don't have my own bank account, or anything. Don't misunderstand me — my Ben never denies me anything. He always says, 'All you have to do is ask.' He gives me everything I want. I never have to ask a second time."

I asked, "Doesn't he have a trust?"

"Not that I know of."

"Does he have a lawyer that I could call?"

"Not that I know of."

"How long have you been married?"

"Two years, next month."

"You said that he was coming home from work. Where does he work?"

"He has car dealerships. I think he was coming home from the one of them the day of the accident."

"And you're sure there is no one who can write a check on his account?"

"Not that I know of."

I was beginning to wonder if there was anything Edeeshia <u>did</u> know. I tried what I thought to be an easy question, "How old a man is your husband?"

She laughed. "He never did tell me his age. I guess he must be close to 60."

"Does he have children from a prior marriage?"

"Yes, his daughter, Debbie."

"Do you think she has access to any of his accounts?"

"I doubt it."

"Did you ask her?"

"No. She hasn't visited much since we married. We never really speak to each other. I mean, it's not that we're mad at each other. We just don't have much in common."

Edeeshia was growing impatient with all the questions, "Can't you just get an order or something so I can get money from the bank account to move him to the nursing home?"

"The nursing home isn't Ben's his only problem. Your husband has many other financial obligations, both personal and business. There are electric bills, water bills, taxes. You need money for food, gas and your general maintenance."

"I can use my credit card."

"But Ben isn't able to pay that credit card each month."

Amazingly, Edeeshia seemed not to have thought of that problem.

I explained, "Unless we can find someone who has Ben's Power of Attorney, we need to ask the Court to appoint you as his Guardian. Once the guardianship is established, you will be able to locate all of his assets and use those assets to pay for his care and for yours."

"I really don't think he gave anyone a Power of Attorney. Let's just go for the guardianship."

We started to fill out the forms. The Court requires that notice of this guardianship proceeding be given to Ben's adult children and his adult siblings, so I'll need their name and address."

"He only has one daughter, that's Debbie and one brother, that's John."

"You may want to call them and tell them to expect to receive notice of the date of the guardianship hearing."

We were able to complete the paper work the next day and I filed the petition. Within the week, I received copies from the court of two other petitions that had been filed. One was a petition to appoint Ben's daughter Debbie as his Guardian. The other was a petition filed by his brother also seeking to be Guardian.

I received a call from Mark Grindell. He had been appointed by the Court to serve as Ben's attorney, "What's going on, Amy? I got a call from the daughter's lawyer and the brother's lawyer. Everyone wants to be Guardian."

"That's what happens when there are big bucks."

"What do we have here, an interracial marriage?"

"Looks that way."

Mark said, "I visited him at the hospital. He's comatose. There is no doubt that he needs a Guardian. But who? The allegations are unbelievable. The lawyer for Ben's daughter, Debbie, says that Edeeshia is a trophy wife who never got past grade school. The lawyer for Ben's brother John, says the same about the wife. He also says that Debbie is a trophy daughter. He said Debbie never worked in her life and to let her handle Ben's money would be a crime. Debbie's lawyer says that Debbie should have priority in appointment because when her father dies all of his money will go to her."

I wondered, "How does Debbie know what she's going to inherit?"

Mark said, "I don't know. I guess I'll have to investigate to see if there is a Will."

"OK. Let me know if you find anything. I'll call my client and ask whether there is a Premarital Agreement that provides for a distribution after Ben's death. If there is, and Edeeshia agrees, I'll make it part of the court record. Meanwhile the hearing is set for Wednesday. I doubt whether the guardianship matter will be decided. Still we can at least have him the Court determine that he is in need of a Guardian."

"Agreed."

Strange how a courtroom takes on the personality of the judge. Judge Stone's courtroom seemed to have a warmth about it. This same room had a whole different feeling with Judge Wecco on the bench. Maybe it was because of a long red plastic line glued to the floor in front of attorney's tables. It looked like one of those lines you see at the Post Office, with a sign in front saying:
WAIT BEHIND THIS LINE FOR THE NEXT CLERK.

The bailiff saw me staring at the line. He whispered to me, "Counselor, you have to stay behind the line. Don't step in front of the line unless you first ask permission." I nodded my head, submissively.

There wasn't enough space at the table for all of the lawyers and their clients, so the lawyers sat at the two tables and their clients occupied the gallery behind them.

After waiting some ten minutes, Judge Wecco, made his grand entrance.

The bailiff bellowed, "All rise."

We stood at attention until the judge took his seat and the bailiff said, "Be seated."

The judge was a portly man, probably in his sixties. He had a very ruddy — almost a flushed appearance. He busily shuffled the petitions before him. He hardly looked up as each attorney took his turn standing and introducing himself and his client.

"Amelia Pohl, your Honor, attorney for Edeeshia Hooper, wife of the alleged incapacitated, Benjamin Hooper."

"Rachael Peterson, attorney for Debbie Hooper, the daughter of the alleged incapacitated."

"Sam Woods, attorney for John Hooper, brother of the alleged incapacitated."

"Mark Grindell, court appointed attorney."

The judge asked, "Mr. Gintlle, do you waive your client's appearance?"

"It's Grindell, your Honor and yes I do. Mr. Hooper is comatose. Has the Court received the Court Investigator's report?"

"Yes, here it is." He looked around the courtroom and asked, "Is there any objection to Mr. Hooper being declared to be in need of a Guardian?"

We all indicated that we had no objection.

"In that case, I declare Benjamin Hooper to be incapacitated and in need of a Guardian." He banged his gavel as if to reinforce his ruling.

The judge turned his attention to the three petitions for guardianship and shook his head, "Three people want to be Guardian. I need more information before I can rule. Mr. Grinchell, have you met with the petitioners?"

"Grin<u>dell</u>, your Honor, and no I have not met any of them.

The lawyers glanced at each other and looked down embarrassed for the judge. What was his problem? Was he deaf? Did he lose his short term memory? His face was very ruddy and he was late entering the court, maybe he was just plain drunk.

The judge seemed not to notice his error and went on, "In that case, Mr. Grinch, I will ask you to meet with each of the petitioners and submit a report to this Court within two weeks with your recommendation for Guardian."

Mark winced. He didn't bother to correct the judge a third time, "Yes, your Honor, I will meet with the parties this week and submit a written report to you."

The judge continued, "I am also instructing the Court Investigator to check the background of each of the three petitioners and make a recommendation as to person best qualified to serve as Guardian. I will see you all back here two weeks from today."

He banged his gavel, stood up and left the court room, barely giving the bailiff time to say "All rise."

I shook my head laughing, "So when are you going to return Christmas, Mr. Grinch?"

"Funny. Very funny," Mark replied. But he was laughing too.

The Court Investigator submitted his report to the Court the following week, with copies to all of the parties. Mark did the same. I was fascinated with what they had to say. The reports read like a novel. It seemed that Ben was 69, closer to 70 than 60, so Edeeshia really didn't know her husband's age.

Debbie was also in the dark when it came to her father. She had no knowledge of how many dealerships he owned. The only one who knew all about Ben was his younger brother, John. They owned two car dealerships together. They each owned other dealerships, individually.

The brothers had been close all of their lives. They attended the same university, both earning degrees in economics. Both married in their 20's. Both eventually divorced. Ben remarried, John remained single. They played golf together at least once a week. John was terribly upset when he heard of the accident. He spent hours at Ben's bedside, talking to him and trying to coax him back to consciousness. He wasn't aware that Edeeshia had no money of her own. When he found out that she had applied for a guardianship in order to pay for Ben's nursing care, John stepped in, wrote out a check and had Ben transferred to a nursing facility.

Debbie was another story. She had been at odds with her father ever since the age of 17, when she became pregnant. The child's father was a drug addict. Debbie was a heavy drinker herself. Luckily, she never got hooked on drugs — but her son did. He was in and out of drug rehabs, and all of it paid by his grandfather. It was true that Debbie never worked a day in her life. Why should she? Her father gave her everything she wanted, and besides, never having completed high school, she was ill equipped to earn a living.

Edeeshia never completed high school either. She became a model when she was in her teens. She was a fast study when it came to clothes, how to walk, how to speak. However, her modeling career faltered when she turned 30. It was rumored that Ben met her when she worked with an "escort service." Debbie was the one who started the rumor, so no one paid much attention to the insinuation.

Debbie was unhappy with Edeeshia from the first day they met. Maybe prejudice, maybe she resented having a step-mother who was younger than she was. More likely she was worried about sharing her inheritance. If her father started a second family, it would be hard for Debbie to compete with cute little half-siblings.

Debbie didn't know that she had little to fear. Ben told his brother that he didn't want to bring a child into this world half black-half white. He didn't think it fair to the child. John suspected it was more that Ben was not too peppy in his old age. Ben struggled just to take care of his businesses each day. He barely had energy for Edeeshia at night. Forget about raising children.

As for Debbie's inheritance, she didn't need to worry about that either. Ben learned well from his divorce from his first wife. He fought bitterly, and still lost half of his wealth to Debbie's mother. He wasn't about to let that happen again. He had one of the best law firms in the county draft a Premarital Agreement. The amount to be inherited by Edeeshia depended on the length of the marriage — 1% of his net worth per year, to a maximum of $100,000. Her inheritance capped at the end of ten years of wedded bliss to one million dollars, or 10% of the value of his net worth — whichever was the lesser value.

No wonder why Edeeshia said she was married two years next month. She was counting the days to her second wedding anniversary.

There are state laws giving a spouse the right to inherit a certain amount from a deceased spouse. In most states that value if one-third of the Estate of the deceased spouse. By signing the Premarital Agreement, Edeeshia gave up all of her marital rights of inheritance. She would have to be married ten years to inherit a very small fraction of what she was entitled to inherit had there been no Premarital Agreement. I wondered if this Agreement was so one-sided as to be unconscionable. That's lawyer talk for "No Court will enforce this Agreement because it's just not fair."

I called Edeeshia and asked whether she had her own attorney represent her during the negotiation leading up to the signing of the Premarital Agreement.

Edeeshia said, "There wasn't any negotiation. Ben said that if I didn't sign, we wouldn't get married. I understood how he felt after what he went through when he divorced his first wife."

"You mean you didn't have an attorney go over this Agreement before you signed it?"

"Ben hired someone for me. The lawyer explained to me what I was signing — but there was no negotiation."

I explained my concerns to Edeeshia, "I want you to meet with a Family Law attorney and see if he thinks you have grounds to challenge the validity of this Premarital Agreement."

"Aren't you sweet to worry about me."

"It's my job to worry about my clients. And speaking of worrying, I need to tell you that I am concerned about the guardianship. The judge might think that John is better qualified to manage Ben's property."

"You mean I won't be in charge of Ben's money?"

"You will be given an allowance each month and we will make sure that it is large enough to continue to maintain you in the life style to which you are accustomed."

The thought of her brother-in-law giving her allowance each month made her teeth clench. In a hard voice — one I'd never heard before, she said, "You don't understand. Ben gave me everything. I was never on an allowance. I don't want to have to ask John for money. No. I want to be Guardian of everything. Tell the judge that we were first to ask to be Guardian and that I am his wife!"

I didn't have the courage to tell Edeeshia that who files the first petition doesn't matter at all. Instead I said, "I understand your position. We already asked the Court to have you appointed Guardian. We already said in the petition that you should be Guardian because you are his wife. We'll just leave our petition as it is. I'll try to persuade the Court Investigator and Ben's court appointed attorney to recommend you as Guardian."

Brian Reilly was the court appointed Investigator. I knew Brian, but only casually. I called him the same day that I spoke to Edeeshia. However, he had already made up his mind. He said John was best qualified to serve as Guardian because of his business savvy and also because he was Ben's brother, and more importantly, his life-long buddy.

Brian thought Debbie irresponsible, and Edeeshia worse, "Edeeshia's spending habits are way over the top. If she were my wife, I would have reined her in a long time ago."

I thought I might have better luck with Mark. I didn't. Mark said, "Edeeshia can't handle his business ventures. Ben owns four dealerships, in addition to the two he partners with his brother. He also has significant real estate holdings and he's very active in the stock market. No. Ben's brother is the logical choice."

"Mark, she is his wife. She should at least have a say as to his medical treatment. You saw that Premarital Agreement. Who better than Edeeshia to make Ben's medical decisions? She has the most to lose if he dies."

He agreed she was the one with most to lose. He said he would talk it over with Brian and see if they could work out a deal for the guardianship of the person.

I told Edeeshia that both the court appointed attorney and the Court Investigator were leaning toward John. "Edeeshia, I don't see how you can compete with John's educational background, and his experience in the very field that Ben earns the majority of his income."

Edeeshia shot back, "Education isn't everything. That's my money!"

I told her that Debbie would probably raise that same argument. "From what we know, Ben doesn't have a Will. You gave up most of your rights in Ben's property, so Debbie is going to say she should be Guardian she's his sole heir. She will say that it's her money and she should have control over how it's spent."

"Debbie? She's dumb as a nail. She'll ruin his business in no time. I'll be penniless in less than a year."

Add to all of this discord, the fact that we had a loose canon on the bench (pardon the pun) and you can imagine my level of anxiety as I waited at the court house for Edeeshia. Having been there once before, I felt I didn't need to accompany Edeeshia to court. I met with her the day before at my office. We discussed the upcoming hearing. I went over her testimony and told her to meet me the next day in the waiting room outside of the courtroom.

Generally, I tell my clients how to dress and how to behave themselves in court. I didn't give Edeeshia any instruction because of the impeccable way she always dressed and the proper way she conducted herself.

I blinked in disbelief when I saw Edeeshia walk into the waiting room. She wore a low-cut, head-turning, blouse, and a short, short, skirt. Her perfume preceded her as she sat down in the seat beside me. I was speechless. So were all of the other attorneys as they entered the waiting room. Only they were silent because they were too busy staring to speak. The staring didn't bother Edeeshia in the least. She had spent most of her life being ogled.

It finally occurred to me what Edeeshia was doing. One thing she knew for sure was SEX SELLS. She was hoping that she could "sell" herself to the judge as the best person to be her husband's Guardian.

It was a strategy, maybe better than mine. The most I could offer was that Edeeshia should have priority in the appointment because she was his spouse, the love of his life, and the one closest to him.

I also knew that there is no priority when it comes to the appointment of a Guardian. The choice of Guardian is strictly up to the judge, and he is guided only by what he perceives to be in the best interest of the Ward.

The judge spotted Edeeshia the minute he entered the court room. In fact, he practically never took his eyes off of her. When she testified, he smiled as if he agreed with her every word. The other attorneys shifted nervously in their seats. They knew the judge's reputation for weird rulings.

After Debbie and John completed their testimony, the lawyers gave their closing arguments. John's lawyer, Sam Woods, was first up. He lifted his head high and practically crowed over the Court Investigator's recommendation that his client be Guardian. Sam said that the Investigator's report was based on solid fact. He read the long list of facts substantiating the Court Investigator's decision. The judge didn't seem to be paying much attention to Sam's lengthy presentation.

As expected, Debbie's lawyer, Rachael, argued that Debbie, as his sole heir, should have control of the finances. It was in her best interest to preserve and protect that money. Rachael argued that Debbie also should serve as Guardian of his person because as his daughter she knew him best. Edeeshia only knew him for a few months before they got married and that was less than two years ago.

When it was my turn, I argued that Debbie had a conflict of interest. True, she was going to be his heir, however she had no money of her own. The sooner her father died, the sooner she could inherit his money.

"My client," I pointed to Edeeshia and the judge smiled again, "has the most to gain to keep her husband alive because the amount she is entitled to inherit depends on the length of their marriage. She is dependent upon her husband for her support, so she also has the most to gain to preserve and protect his property."

Mark, as the court appointed attorney, gave his closing argument on behalf of Ben. He agreed with the Court Investigator. The only one qualified to serve as Guardian of the Ward's property was his brother John. Mark said, "As for Guardian of the person, I agree with Mrs. Pohl, the daughter does have a conflict of interest and Mrs. Hooper has the most to gain from keeping her husband alive. However, based on the long standing relationship between the Ward and his brother, John Hooper is my choice to serve as Guardian of the person, as well."

At the end of Mark's closing argument, we all turned our attention to the judge. He shuffled the papers in front of him for a few minutes. He seemed to think for another few minutes and then said, "I will take this matter under advisement."

He got up and walked out of the court room.

Edeeshia asked "What happened?"

I explained, "It just means that the judge is going to think about it and make his ruling later on."

"When?" Edeeshia wanted to know.

Mark answered, "He'll probably mail the order to us within the week."

When I saw the letter from the Court, I could hardly wait to open it. I ripped open the envelop. True to his reputation for rulings sure to offend everyone, Judge Wecco appointed Debbie as the Guardian to manage Ben's property and Edeeshia as Guardian for Ben's personal needs!

I called Edeeshia with the news. She was not happy. She questioned whether the arrangement would work. "How can I take care of Ben if I don't have any money? That's why I started this whole thing in the first place."

I explained that as Guardian of Ben's property, Debbie was required to make funds available for his care.

Edeeshia said, "What about my care? Is she going to make money available for me?"

"Yes. As Guardian she is required to use Ben's money to provide support for those who dependent on the Ward for their support. She should continue to pay for all of your household expenses, as well as your credit card bills. Let's see how Debbie performs her duties as the Guardian of his property. If things don't work out, we can always petition the Court for relief."

Chapter 3a   The Battling Guardians

Sam Woods, John's attorney, was on the phone the same day I received the order. He was calling the other attorneys to get their reaction to the appointment. He confided that he did little guardianship work and that the judge's ruling was a complete surprise.

"Experience has nothing to do with it," I said, "we all were surprised."

Sam said he was considering appealing the judge's decision. I advised against it. "Sam, you can look up the case law. Guardianship decisions are rarely overturned. The choice of Guardian is strictly up to the judge. In this case, he based his decision on the fact that Debbie is Ben's sole heir, so it's her money anyway. If you research the topic, I think you'll find that there the judge was justified in appointing her Guardian of her father's property."

"What about Ben's partnership interest in my client's dealership? He can't have Debbie as a partner. That would ruin his business!"

"I agree. Maybe you can ask the Court that John be appointed as the Guardian of Ben's partnership interest only, and just limit John's guardianship to the partnership interest."

Sam asked, "Do you think that will work?"

"I don't know. It seems like a reasonable solution, however, I've never seen such an arrangement. Why don't you ask Mark? He's still Ben's attorney and he did recommend John as Guardian."

I received a copy of Sam's petition to appoint John as Guardian of Ben's partnership interest. I would like to have seen a Memorandum of Law attached to the petition explaining that this was permissible under the law. Judge Wecco, being new to the Probate Division, didn't have enough background to know whether this was an acceptable guardianship practice. Unless Sam came to the hearing with case law to back him, I doubted whether the petition would fly as it was written. And it didn't. I received a copy of the order denying the petition.

I wasn't present at the hearing for John's petition because it didn't affect Edeeshia's role as Guardian of Ben's person. Still, I wondered what had happened at the hearing, so when I met Mark at the monthly New York Bar luncheon, I asked for the details. He said, "Wecco practically threw the petition back at Sam. He told him 'If your client doesn't want Ms. Hooper to manage the Ward's partnership interest, he can buy out the Ward's interest, or he can sell his own interest to the Ward.'"

The brother chose the former, leaving Debbie with a pile of cash that she probably had no idea how to invest. I called Debbie's attorney, Rachael. "Edeeshia is concerned about the way Debbie is managing Ben's money. She has no financial background. Has she employed a trust company or a financial planner to help her?"

Rachael didn't know. She said that she would ask Debbie and get back to me. She didn't. Two weeks later I called her once again. Rachael said that her client felt she was perfectly capable of handling Ben's money and she didn't need a trust company telling her what to do.

I called Mark and told him about the problem. He agreed that we couldn't wait a year to see what Debbie was doing with the money.

We drafted a joint petition asking the Court to order that Debbie employ a trust company to manage Ben's considerable fortune. We attached a Memorandum of Law to the petition explaining the Guardian's fiduciary duty to the Ward to preserve and protect his assets. In the absence of a financial background, the Guardian was required to employ persons experienced in money management. The Memorandum included a summary of Debbie's educational background. Her poor grades in high school and the fact that she had to repeat algebra, as well as geometry, showed that she was ill equipped to manage her father's property.

Finally! The judge did something reasonable. He ruled in our favor and ordered Debbie to employ a trust company to manage the guardianship funds.

The next battle was over the matter of Edeeshia's maintenance. Debbie had been paying all of the house expenses, as well as Edeeshia's credit card balance each month. She didn't question how much Edeeshia was spending. I suspected it was because Debbie was spending so on herself that she didn't want to bring up the issue of Edeeshia's maintenance. Debbie knew that if the matter came before the Court, I would be sure to reveal how much she was taking each month.

Things changed once the trust company took over. The trust officer in charge of monthly expenses tried to put both Debbic and Edeeshia on a budget. Naturally it was for an amount much less than what they had been spending.

This time I filed a joint petition with Rachael. We asked the Court to set the amount each would receive each month as maintenance.

The amount requested was considerably higher than the trust officer thought it should be, so he had the vice president of his company testify at the court hearing as to the average maintenance costs in other trusts of this size.

Judge Wecco awarded an amount close to what the women were asking, however he issued a stern warning, "This is the third time you Guardians have been before this Court. If you all can't handle this guardianship without constantly petitioning this Court, I'll find someone who can!"

Within the month Edeeshia was on the phone. She was upset with the nursing home and felt Ben wasn't getting the kind of care he deserved. "They aren't doing anything for Ben. He just lies there. I heard about this hospital that is doing experimental work on people in a coma. They are trying something called 'stimulation therapy.' They play the patient's favorite music. They massage the patient three times a day and try to get him to sit up. They even give him aroma therapy. The idea is to stimulate the whole brain to help the patient to wake up."

I agreed, "That sounds like a good idea. As Guardian for his personal needs, you have the right to direct his medical care."

"The problem is that it cost a lot of money each month to give him that kind of care. Debbie says that she's the Guardian of his property and she refuses to use guardianship funds to pay for it."

I called Debbie's lawyer to see if we could resolve the matter. Rachael said that Debbie was adamant in her refusal to pay for the treatment.

Debbie said there was no point in spending that kind of money on an unproven treatment. Edeeshia was equally adamant, so we set the matter for a hearing.

The hearing on the matter of Ben's transfer to the experimental treatment facility was lengthy with numerous witnesses. Debbie testified that the experimental facility was over 60 miles from her home. It would be a hardship to travel that far to visit him. I countered the argument by producing records from the nursing home showing that Debbie's visits were infrequent, averaging once every two months — even though her home is only five miles from his current nursing home.

Debbie's lawyer had Ben's treating physician testify that Ben was essentially brain dead. He said that in his very lengthy practice he had never seen anyone come out such a deep coma. He felt it would not be in the best interest of his patient to subject him to this kind of disruptive and uncomfortable therapy. Only he used the word "torture."

I brought in the doctor in charge of the experimental treatment facility. He had a different story to tell. They were getting good results with stimulation therapy. However, on Rachael's cross examination he admitted that the best results were those closest to the time of the accident. "That doesn't mean there is no hope of recovery," the doctor said.

"Yes, miracles do happen," Rachael replied sarcastically.

Closing arguments were particularly nasty. Rachael said Edeeshia had nothing but hard feelings for Debbie and was trying to spend as much of Ben's money as possible just for spite.

I argued that Edeeshia was trying everything in her power to bring Ben back to health. Debbie had no such motivation. She would be one wealthy heiress once her father was dead.

Mark was there at the hearing, however he did not express an opinion one way or the other, "I defer to the sound discretion of the Court," he said.

The judge didn't appear to be paying much attention to the hearing. It seemed to me that he made up his mind after reading our petitions and Memorandum of Law. Probably the petitions made him see the foolishness of his appointment of one Guardian to care for the person of the Ward and another to care for the property of the Ward. That arrangement could never work when the two Guardians are at odds with each other.

I guessed right because at the end of the hearing the judge said, "I am removing both of you as Guardian. You are each ineligible because of a conflict of interest. Mrs. Hooper, your fortunes rest on how long you can keep your husband alive — even if it means subjecting him to experimental treatment that may cause him significant discomfort. Ms. Hooper, your conflict of interest is obvious. The sooner your father dies, the sooner you inherit his Estate. I am appointing a professional Guardian to serve as the Guardian of the person and the property of the Ward."

He said to me, "Mrs. Pohl, have Mrs. Hooper submit her final report, giving her opinion as to the best method of treatment and the best facility for her husband. The successor Guardian will review the report and make an independent decision about his treatment and nursing care facility."

The judge turned to Rachael, "Have your client submit a final accounting within ten days. I'll be appointing a professional Guardian within the week. Notify the trust company that the successor Guardian will be in charge of paying for the care of the Ward."

Edeeshia was confused. As soon as we were out of the courtroom she asked, "What did he say?"

I explained, "He removed both you and Debbie as Guardians because he felt you each had a conflict of interest. He's appointing a professional Guardian to care for Ben and his property."

Edeeshia asked, "What's a professional Guardian?"

"Generally, it is someone who earns a living as Guardian.

"You mean someone who is licensed as a Guardian?"

"No. In many states, including this one, there are no licensing or even educational requirements for a professional Guardians."

Edeeshia was surprised, "You mean the judge can ask anyone he wants to be Ben's Guardian without even checking his background?"

"He could. We have no law in this state requiring a criminal or background check. The judge will probably order a bond, so if the Guardian turns out to be dishonest, the guardianship Estate will be protected."

Edeeshia was angry, "What gives him the right to remove us and appoint some stranger without even asking us who we want to be Guardian?"

"He's the judge. Whoever he says is Guardian, is Guardian. Still he did warn you. Don't you remember at the hearing for your monthly maintenance when he said he was going to get another Guardian if you kept pestering the Court? Only he didn't say 'pestering' he said 'petitioning' the Court. To him, it's the same thing."

"Yeah, but I didn't think he would."

What Edeeshia, Debbie and John all learned the hard way, is that when it comes to a guardianship, you are indeed at the mercy of the Court.

The Contested Capacity Hearing 4

I'm not very good at names. Especially if the name doesn't fit my preconceived idea of what that name should look like. As soon as I met Barbara, I knew I would have no problem remembering her name. To me, she was the quintessential Barbara. Tall, light wavy hair, fair skin and a pleasant countenance.

"It's my Uncle Frank. He has ALS. You know the one where they slowly can't move any more. Lou Gehrig had it."

I nodded, "The scientist, Stephen Hawking, has it too."

"Yeah, I saw him on T.V. Only he uses a computer to speak. Uncle Frank can still talk, but he can't walk. He has been living with me for the past two years. We have a nurse come in twice once a week to give him a baths and check his blood pressure. Mostly I take care of him."

"That must be a full time job."

"Yes. He pays me well. He's very generous."

"Is he still able to sign checks?"

"No. We have a joint account, and he has money transferred into that account so I can pay for his food, medicine, and to pay me for taking care of him."

I asked, "How does the money get transferred into the account?"

"Well, that's the problem. He gave his Power of Attorney to Manny, who Uncle Frank calls his financial advisor. Manny used it to transfer all of Uncle Frank's money into his own name. We're worried he's going to take off with Uncle Frank's money."

"Who's 'we'?"

"The whole family, my mother, my brother, my sister. We're all worried about Uncle Frank."

"This sounds like a case of exploitation of the elderly. Did you call the state Department of Aging?"

Barbara said, "Yes, I did. They sent out an investigator who spoke to Uncle Frank. The investigator said that Uncle Frank knew exactly how much money he had. He knew that Manny was keeping the money in a brokerage account in Manny's name. He said it was just easier for Manny to trade in his own name than being required to produce the Power of Attorney every time he wanted to make a trade. Manny showed all of his records to the investigator. They said the records agreed with the amount of money Uncle Frank said he had. "

I asked, "And how much is that?"

"About $800,000."

"The investigator said there wasn't anything she could do. Uncle Frank said he wants Manny to keep the money in that brokerage account, so there was no way to file criminal charges against Manny."

I asked whether there was any written report from the investigator saying that Uncle Frank was in need of a Guardian.

Barbara said, "No. I have a copy of her report here. All it says is that she didn't find any evidence of a crime. The investigator did tell me that she thought Uncle Frank was using very bad judgment in his dealings with Manny. She said she thought Manny was taking advantage of Uncle's Frank's weakened condition. She thought that my uncle is losing it, mentally. She was the one to suggest we get the Court to appoint a Guardian for him. That's why I'm here."

"Did she put any of that in writing?"

"No," Barbara said.

"Do you have any report from a doctor saying that your uncle can't manage his medical treatment."

"No. But he can't. I make all of his medical decisions. I do all of the talking to the doctor. And he's not making any of his business decisions. Manny is doing all of that. Uncle Frank says he knows what's going on. He doesn't. I asked him what would happen to the money in Manny's account if he died. He said that Manny would give it to the family according to the directions in my uncle's Will. That's the same Will he gave to Manny for safe keeping. Does that make any sense to you?"

I had to agree that it didn't. However, knowing that a family member is losing it, and proving it, are two different things. "Everyone is free to make bad judgments. And we all do that from time to time. To get a Guardian appointed for your uncle, we'll need to prove to the Court that he doesn't know what he's doing. That may be hard to do."

I wondered, "Is there any chance your Uncle will agree to allow you to be his Guardian?"

"No way. Uncle Frank thinks he's fine. He would never want a Court to decide that he doesn't know what he's doing. He's is a proud man. He'll fight a guardianship as hard as he can."

I almost didn't take the case. I dreaded the thought of arguing a contested capacity hearing before Wecco. Then I realized I would have to argue all of my guardianship cases before this judge for the next five years. May as well learn to deal with his erratic ways. The only other alternative was to give up my guardianship practice altogether, and I wasn't about to do that.

I showed Barbara the Petition To Appoint a Guardian. "You need to complete this form. You'll need to state the facts on which you base your belief that your uncle is in need of a Guardian. It is good practice to attach letters to the petition substantiating those facts. It will be a big help if you can get the investigator to agree to sign an *Affidavit* (a statement sworn to under oath) stating how she came to the conclusion that he needs a Guardian. We also need an Affidavit from his doctor saying that your uncle doesn't have the ability to make his medical decisions. You should also have a psychologist examine your uncle and give his opinion about whether Frank is able to handle his finances."

"If we have a psychologist examine Uncle Frank, he will find out what we're doing."

"He will anyway. State law requires that he be served with a Notice that gives the date of the guardianship hearing together with a copy of your petition."

I suggested, "Telling him up front is the best approach. It might be a good idea to arrange a family meeting with him. Something like the interventions you see on T.V. when the family is trying to get an addict to rehab. You'll need to explain to him why you are concerned. Lean heavily on the recommendation of the investigator. Tell him that you are only doing what she suggested and that she is an experienced investigator and knows when someone needs a Guardian. Explain that he can still have Manny as his financial advisor, the only difference is that his money will be protected in a guardianship account."

Barbara called me the next week, "The family meeting didn't go over too good. Uncle Frank got very angry. He said he was going to disinherit all of us. Can he do that?"

"If the Court finds your uncle is incapacitated, he may order Manny to turn your uncle's Will over to the Court. Once your uncle dies, there's a good chance the probate judge will find that any Will written after that one to be invalid. Still I have to warn you. If the Court finds that your uncle is able to care for himself and his property, he will be free to leave all of his money to Manny. If a Guardian is not appointed, you will not be reimbursed for any of the money you are spending. You could be out thousands of dollars. Maybe you should try to get letters from the investigator, the psychologist and the doctor before you make a final decision about pursuing this guardianship."

She thought that was a good idea and said she would get back to me.

I had almost forgotten about the case when I got a call from Barbara some three weeks later.

"My family wants me to try to become Guardian. Everyone is going to chip in to pay the legal costs. They feel if we don't do something, Uncle Frank will lose all of his money for sure. We don't have a choice. We need to at least try to protect him. I have the letter from the investigator, and the letter from his doctor. My uncle wouldn't talk to the psychologist we hired. The doctor did agree to wrote an opinion letter based on what we told him, and the way Uncle Frank acted when he tried to talk to him, so I have the three letters."

"OK. make an appointment with my secretary to come in and complete the petition."

I filed the petitions with the court. Within the week I received a call from Rachael Peterson, the same attorney who had represented Debbie in the Hooper case. Rachael told me that she was going to defend Frank at the guardianship hearing.

"You mean Frank came to your office and asked you to be his lawyer?"

Rachael stammered a bit, "Well, no. Frank isn't mobile. Manny called me. He used Frank's Power of Attorney to employ me and sign a retainer agreement on behalf of Frank. I did meet Frank. He absolutely does not want a Guardian. I was just calling to let you know that I filed a Notice of Appearance as Frank's lawyer and to ask whether you knew who Wecco appointed as the Court Investigator."

"No. I haven't heard anything. Now that you filed a Notice of Appearance, the Clerk will send you a copy of his report."

I had mixed feelings when I hung up the phone. Rachael was a no nonsense attorney, often acting tougher than she needed. Then again, arguing the Hooper case before Wecco had been a humbling experience for her. In the end, her client was dismissed as Guardian and so was mine. We both knew that the only thing you could expect from Wecco was the unexpected. We would both tread gingerly in this case.

I called Barbara and told her that Manny employed Rachael to represent Frank. "Rachael filed a Notice of Appearance with the Court."

"What's that?"

I explained, "A Notice of Appearance is a document that an attorney files with the Court to let the Court know that she is representing a party to an action that is presently before the Court."

Barbara wanted to know how this affected the case, "Is that bad?"

"Not bad, just a bit more difficult. If Frank hadn't employed a lawyer, the Court would have chosen a lawyer to represent him at the hearing. A lawyer appointed by the Court is there to represent Frank, however, as a Court appointment he is also concerned with the best interests of his client. He may be more objective in his assessment of the situation than an attorney employed by Frank — or in this case, Manny."

I explained, "Rachael was employed by Manny to prevent a Guardian from being appointed. She's not going to wonder whether that may not be in Frank's best interest. So far as she is concerned, it's her job to show that he doesn't need a Guardian. She considers it to be my job to show that he does."

The following week I received a copy of Court Investigator's report. He said that Frank had a misguided sense of his own ability to comprehend financial matters. In his opinion, Frank did not understand the consequences of such inability, so he recommended the appointment of a Guardian to manage Frank's property. The Investigator also determined that Frank had little understanding of the nature of his illness. He doubted whether Frank was able to make meaningful decisions regarding his health care. He recommended the appointment of a Guardian for Frank's personal needs.

I mailed copies of the Court Investigator's report to Barbara. When she called I could hear the smile in her voice. "He's in favor of a Guardian for Uncle Frank's personal needs and to manage his property. I never expected the results to be this good."

I wasn't as optimistic, "If it were up to the Court Investigator to decide, you would soon be Guardian. But it's up to the judge. I know from past experience, Judge Wecco rules as he sees fit. I have seen him completely disregard a report submitted by the Court Investigator."

The week prior to the hearing was spent preparing myself and my client for court.

I needed to have Barbara come across as a loving niece whose only concern was the well being of her uncle. I knew that appearances would play a part in Judge Wecco's decision, so I made sure her hair, makeup and clothing were attractive. I had her dress in a conservative business suit to suggest that she was able to handle her uncle's finances.

I prepared the rest of the family in the same way — properly dressed, whose only concern was the well being of their loved one. Luckily, there was a long history of a close familial relationship, so that wasn't hard to do.

Rachael planned to call Manny as a witness. I did a background check on him. Nothing came up. He had no criminal record. He never filed for bankruptcy. None the less, I believed Manny to be a con artist. I expected that Manny would come across as a really nice guy, whose only motive was to help a dear friend who was becoming increasingly disabled. I hoped to show through clever cross examination that Manny was taking advantage of Frank's weakness to make Frank act in Manny's best interest and not the way Frank would have acted had he not been ill. In legal terms that's called *undue influence*, and it's against the law.

Clever cross exam or no, showing undue influence was a long shot. Every con artist I ever met comes across as totally trustworthy. That's why they are so good at what they do. Con artists have the ability to disarm the alarm system in your brain that is supposed to yell "Thief, thief" when you are in the presence of someone who is about to relieve you of your life savings.

No. The most I could realistically hope to accomplish was to get Manny to admit that keeping Frank's money in his own account violated the ethics of his own community of financial advisors.

I planned to spend considerable time cross examining Frank. I knew from speaking with the Court Investigator that initially Frank comes across as knowing what he's doing. The Court Evaluator said "After 15 or 20 minutes, he tires. His memory slips. His comments become less rational." I hoped to cross examine Frank long enough to get him to that point of irrationality.

I knew Rachael would talk about the Will. I was sure she would say that this hearing was not about Frank's capacity, but just a way to make sure that the family inherited his wealth. To counter this argument, I needed to get Frank to say that he had always wanted to have his family inherit his wealth. I needed him to say that he believed it was a good idea to have Manny in possession of his Will, and in personal possession of all of his money. And if the judge didn't notice that this financial arrangement made no sense, I planned to say in my closing argument that only a man with diminished capacity would make such arrangements.

I spent a lot of time preparing for the hearing. What I wasn't prepared for was Frank. He was wheeled into the courtroom. I have never seen a man so completely disabled. He sat crunched down in his wheel chair, hands folded awkwardly on his lap. He was barely able to keep his head upright. He had difficulty swallowing his saliva. His nurse wiped his chin as it seeped out of the corner of his mouth. He sat quietly in his wheelchair while I put on my case and Rachael put on hers. Good lawyer that she was, she saved Frank's testimony for last.

The nurse wheeled Frank up to the witness chair. His voice was so weak, she had to hold the microphone close to his lips.

Frank first complained about the hearing itself. "This hearing is embarrassing. I know what I look like. Do I have to be exposed to all of you starring at me? Bad enough not having any control of my body. Do I have to listen to a bunch of so called experts saying that I don't have any control over my mind as well? There's nothing wrong with me. I know what I am doing. I have a good memory. I know my family cares for me. Barbara has been very good to me. I know I'm a lot of work. I appreciate everything she does for me. Any other family would dump me in a nursing home. Not my family. I know they love me and I love them. It's just they treat me like a child. They talk about me like I'm not in the room, 'Did the doctor see Frank today?' Why don't they ask me, 'Did you see the doctor today?' I'm not senile. I have feelings."

His anger seemed to overwhelm him. He seemed out of breath. The nurse gave him a sip of water and he was able to continue, "I know Manny a long time — before I got this sick. He always made good investments for me. I always trusted him. My portfolio would not be this big, if it weren't for him. He talks <u>with</u> me, not about me. He treats me like a man. Of course I let him keep the money under his name. And I asked him to hold on to my Will. Why not? He's the one who is going to be my Personal Representative. I trust him. I love him. He's like a son to me."

Tears rolled down Frank's face. He was unable to go on.

No way was I going to get a chance to cross examine him this day.

The judge was visibly moved by Frank's testimony. He took a break in the proceeding and called me and Rachael into his chambers. "Ms. Peterson, has your client considered giving his niece a voluntary guardianship?"

A *voluntary guardianship*? I couldn't believe my ears! "Your Honor, what you are proposing is just the same as giving my client a Power of Attorney. Once appointed, Mr. Davis would be free at any time to ask the Court to discharge her as Guardian. Respectfully, judge, I don't see how that could solve anything unless you revoked Manny's Power of Attorney and had all of the money Manny keeps in the brokerage account transferred to a guardianship account."

"That would be up to Mr. Davis. I'm not going to rule today. You girls work out a proposed order and submit it to my office."

YOU GIRLS??? What were we? School children being told by the playground teacher to play nice together?

I made a fast exit out of the room before I said things that could land me in jail for contempt of Court — if not debarred.

The slight did not bother Rachael in the least. She won! There would be no ruling that Frank was in needed of a Guardian in Judge Wecco's courtroom.

Chapter 4a The Voluntary Guardianship

The following week Rachael filed a petition on behalf of Frank asking the Court to appoint Barbara as the Guardian of the joint account that was already in both their names. The petition requested that Barbara use the money in the joint account to pay for the maintenance of the Ward and that Barbara be subject to the same duties and responsibilities as provided by law for a Guardian of the property.

I was on the phone as soon I received a copy of the Petition, "Rachael, how is my client supposed to give an annual accounting of transactions from their joint account when she has no control over the amount of money going into the account?"

"OK. I'll amend the petition to reflect that she only needs to account for withdrawals from the account."

"That helps, but it doesn't solve the problem. Why don't you put in a petition to have Manny be appointed as Guardian of Frank's brokerage account? At least we'll have Court supervision of what Manny does with Frank's money."

Rachael said she already thought of that and suggested it to Frank. He talked it over with Manny, however Manny refused. "Manny said that being Frank's Guardian would change their relationship. He said he wanted to keep their friendship on an equal basis. If he were a Guardian he would be in charge of Frank and they neither wanted that."

"And Frank bought that?"

"Of course."

I could hear in Rachael's voice that she understood Manny's true intentions, so I persisted, "Can't you tell Frank that this would be a voluntary guardianship and that he could terminate the guardianship any time he wishes. It's really no different than the Power of Attorney that he gave to Manny."

"Manny's wouldn't agree to that. He's a smart guy. He knows the difference between a Power of Attorney and a voluntary guardianship. He knows that if he's appointed Guardian, he'd have to account to the Court each year. Apparently, he's not willing to do that."

I had to admit she was right, "I guess all we can do is get Barbara to serve as Guardian of the joint account. At least by having Barbara appointed Guardian, Frank will pick up all of the attorney fees and court costs and Barbara won't be out any money."

"Exactly," said Rachael.

I called Barbara into my office and explained the voluntary guardianship to her. She was angry and rightly so. She said, "This doesn't solve a damn thing. Manny gets to keep the brokerage account in his name. If he hasn't already, he will be sure to get Uncle Frank to change his Will and leave all he owns to Manny. That judge is a jackass. How can he ignore the report of the Court Investigator who he appointed? "

"I think the judge was swayed by Frank's testimony. Your uncle did come across as if he knew what he was saying."

Barbara was well aware of what happened. "What did he testify? A big five minutes? If he had continued for another ten or fifteen minutes, the judge would have seen that Frank doesn't know what he's talking about. How could that judge compare five minutes in court with the hours spent by the Court Investigator? My uncle didn't fool him."

I offered Barbara hope for future action, "Frank's disease is progressive. It's going to get to the point where he won't be able to speak any more. That can't be far down the road. As soon as he is no longer able to communicate, you can put in another petition. The judge will have no choice but to find him to be in need of a Guardian."

Barbara was satisfied with the thought that she still had a chance at saving Uncle Frank's $800,000, so she accepted the voluntary guardianship.

Our hope for future action was short lived.Within the week Barbara was on the phone. "Manny's taking Uncle Frank to Bermuda. He says Uncle Frank needs a vacation. He says they'll be back in two weeks. But I don't trust him."

I agreed, "Tell Manny you have to go along so that you can take care of your Uncle."

"No. Manny already arranged for a full time nurse. He says he has first class seats on the airplane and that they leave tomorrow morning. He told Uncle Frank that this vacation is a celebration for the victory they had in court."

I became apprehensive when I realized what was happening. No doubt Manny figured out the same thing I did. He knew that Frank would soon be too sick to talk and that it was only a matter of time before Barbara would be back in court seeking a full guardianship. By taking Frank out of the country he was making sure that he stayed in control until Frank died.

I told Barbara that it was imperative to get the whole family together and do everything they could to stop that trip.

Barbara and her family did exactly what I suggested and more so. They called the police. Once again, Frank was able to convince the powers that be that he was in control of his faculties. He said that he was a grown man and resented his family treating him like a child. He said he really wanted to take a vacation. He told the police that he had been to court and the judge found him to be competent to take care of himself.

Unfortunately, Barbara and her family had to admit to the police that Judge Wecco did indeed deny their petition to be appointed as Guardian of his person.

The police left and so did Uncle Frank.

Manny took Frank (and his $800,000) to Bermuda, and then to the Virgin Islands and then to Nicaragua, and then to who knows where.

After a few weeks, Barbara filed a missing person report, however neither Uncle Frank nor Manny were ever heard from again.

The Gift Giving Ward 5

From as early as she could remember, Consuela wanted to go to the United States. She was a mediocre student at best, yet when it came to learning English, she was a natural. Her friends called her "the little American."

She was 17 when her boyfriend said he was going to try to cross the border into Texas. She begged to go with him. The trip to the states was short. They were picked up just outside the Mexican border, fingerprinted, photographed and then turned over to Mexican authorities.

A few months later, she broke off the relationship with her boyfriend when she found him in the embrace of another woman. More than ever, Consuela wanted to leave Mexico and go to America. She decided to join a group who were going to try a path through the dessert. That decision almost cost her life. They got lost in the dessert. After a few days of wandering without food or water, she was more than happy to be picked up by a U.S. border patrol. Once again she was fingerprinted, photographed and sent back to Mexico.

After that frightening experience, Consuela resigned herself to remain in Mexico. She got a job as housekeeper to a wealthy family. They were very kind to her. Still the desire to go to American never left her.

As she and her employers came to know each other, Consuela told them about her failed attempts to enter the states, "There's nothing here for me. Just a lifetime of scrubbing floors. In America, I could be somebody." Her employers understood and were sympathetic to Consuela's hope and ambition. The wife said, "You worked too hard trying to cross the border. There's an easy way. I have a brother who lives in Bayou La Batrie. That's in Alabama. Once a year he takes his boat on a cruise to visit us in Mexico. The next time he visits, we'll ask him to take you back to the United States in his ship. You can enter the States first class!"

The brother turned out to be just as kind and sympathetic as her employers. Not only did he take her to Alabama, once they docked, he put her on a bus to Miami, where she could seek out one of her cousins.

Consuela knew she would be safe in Miami. With her Spanish accent, dark eyes, dark hair and tan skin, she blended right into with the general population. It wasn't long before Connie (as she came to be known) met and married a handsome fellow of Spanish descent. They settled down and had a boy and a girl.

Maybe Connie was just unlucky in love, or maybe she, as so many woman do, become involved with the same kind of guy, over and over again. Just like her Mexican boy friend, her husband had a wandering eye. Connie couldn't understand why he wanted to be with other women. She knew she was attractive. She was well endowed by nature. The size of her endowment was accented by her thin waist and short stature. No. If her husband felt the need to chase other woman, it was his problem, and one she would not tolerate. She took the children and left.

Being unskilled and having the additional handicap of being an illegal alien, the best she work she could find was cleaning houses. Arthur was one of her first customers.

Arthur was an elderly widower. He had recently been diagnosed as having Parkinson's disease. The doctor didn't tell him much about what to expect as the disease progressed, so Arthur research the Internet. He found the symptoms he could expect as the disease progressed:

Tremor Yes. His hands shook. It was hard for him to write. That's what brought him to the doctor.

Shuffling Gait Yes. He couldn't lift his feet as he walked.

Rigidity Yes. He had stiffness. It was hard for him to move. When he did move, he had to move slowly.

Facial Masking Inability to use muscles in the face, with resulting loss of facial expression.
Arthur didn't think he had this symptom yet. He looked in the mirror and smiled just to be sure.

Arthur was not yet experiencing all of the other symptoms listed on the Internet:
loss of smell, loss of ability to speak, bladder problems, sexual disfunction, sleep problems, constipation, falling, fainting, difficulty swallowing, dementia.

'Dementia?' He thought, 'My God, this is worse than Alzheimer's. At least with Alzheimer's, all you lose is your memory!'

Arthur had been a strong, active, man all of his life. The thought of being alone and so completely disabled was frightening.

He tried to fight the disease and keep mobile, however the tremors made it difficult to do the simplest thing. He took medication which gave him temporary relief. He felt sad — no depressed, most of the time. He didn't know if it was a side effect of the medicine or just knowing where this disease was headed.

It was a struggle to keep his apartment clean. One of his neighbors suggested Arthur employ a house cleaner. He recommended a woman who was cleaning apartments in the condo complex.

The first time he met Connie, Arthur's world brightened. Just looking at her made him smile. She not only cleaned his house, she spent time visiting with him. They had much in common. His mother was also from Mexico. They spent hours talking in a mixture of English and Spanish. It wasn't long before Arthur became Connie's full time job.

Arthur appreciated everything Connie did for him and paid her generously. He even proposed marriage, but she never divorced her husband, and had no intention of doing so. She made it clear that sex was not part of their business arrangement. Arthur professed his love for her, however as he became increasingly disabled, he knew that sex was just another thing he would need to do without.

Arthur had a daughter, Isabella, who lived in New York. Though she rarely visited, she was well aware of the relationship between Arthur and Connie. And she did not like it. When Arthur told his daughter that he bought a car for Connie, she was sure that his Parkinson's was affecting his mind. She felt she had to move quickly or Connie would soon have all his money. She called the state Department of Aging.

That's how I came to meet Arthur. He called and said that Department was doing an investigation, "Do I have to talk to them? What can they do to me if I don't?"

There was no way to answer the question until I determined his degree of impairment and the circumstances leading up to the investigation, so I asked him to come in for an appointment.

Connie wheeled Arthur into my office. I asked her to go to the waiting room while I consulted with my client. Arthur objected, "I have no secrets from Connie. I want her to stay right here with me."

I explained about the attorney client relationship, "If Connie remains in the room, anything you say to me will not be confidential. That might be a real problem during this investigation."

Connie said, "It's OK. I'll be right outside. You can tell me what the lawyer said later."

Although his dependence on Connie was obvious, he seemed to have all of his faculties. "My daughter started all this. She's only interested in my money. She never did anything for me. My daughter never helped me when I was taking care of her mother before she died. I needed help then, but Isabella was always too busy with her own life. Connie takes good care of me. I bought the car so she could use it to take me shopping and to the doctor. It has a special lift for my wheelchair. "

I asked, "Why did you put the car in her name?"

"I wanted her to have it in case something happens to me."

I suggested that it might have been better had he put the car in both names, "You could have titled the car so that Connie would not be able to sell it during your lifetime without your signature. Once you die, it would have gone to Connie, automatically. By titling the car in that manner, there would have been no question to raise with the Department of Aging."

Arthur said he wished he had consulted with me earlier. "What do we do now?"

I suggested that we set up a meeting with the Department investigator here in my office. I knew once he met with Connie and Arthur, he would find that Arthur was not being exploited. Connie was taking good care of him. There was nothing wrong with him buying a car that was needed for his care and putting it in her name on it in the event he died.

Before setting up the meeting I wanted to be sure there were no other issues I needed to know about, "Did you give Connie other gifts?"

"Yes, I gave her earrings and a matching necklace for Christmas, and I gave her children toys. I pay her for taking care of me. She does that eight hours a day, every day. Saturday, Sunday, holidays. I pay her well because she deserves it!"

I told Arthur that the investigator would want to review his bank records to verify that Connie was not taking money from his account. He said that only his name was on his bank account, and he only gave her money for the work she did. He offered to send me a copy of those records which he did the next day.

I interviewed Connie separately. She told much the same story. From all that I had learned, I felt comfortable that investigator would close the case with a finding that there was no indication of exploitation.

And that's exactly what happened.

Several months later I received a call from Arthur, "My Parkinson's is getting worse. I'm getting to the point that I need 24 hour care. If I had a bigger house, Connie and her children could come to live with me. Connie wants me to put the house in her name in exchange for taking care of me until I die."

I could almost hear horns and whistles — like a car alarm when someone tries to get in without a key.

I asked, "Did you buy the house yet?"

"No, but we have one that we picked out."

"Good. I want you to come to my office before you do anything."

Connie wheeled Arthur into my office. She wanted to stay in the room while I spoke to Arthur. Once again, I explained about the attorney client relationship. Only this time Connie was insistent, "We're going to buy the house together, so I should be here."

"No. I'm Arthur's attorney. I do not represent you. In fact, if you are going to buy a house together, I recommend you employ your own attorney to represent you. Right now I need to talk to Arthur alone."

Hearing the resolve in my voice, Arthur told Connie to wait outside, "I'll tell you what we said later."

"Arthur, this is not a good idea. If your daughter finds out that you bought a house and put it in Connie's name, she will go right back to the Department of Aging. Your condition is worse than when I last saw you. This time the investigator might decide that Connie is exploiting you. "

"I need someone to take care of me. I don't want to die in some nursing home, by myself. I want Connie to stay with me. "

I explained that there were other ways to accomplish that goal. "You and Connie could sign an employment contract. She gets the house in exchange for taking care of you till you die. She doesn't get the house till she fills her end of the bargain."

"No. I don't think Connie would go for that. What if she can't take care of me for some reason — then she doesn't get the house?"

I said firmly, "That's the whole point of the contract. Would you want her to get the house if she didn't take care of you? "

Arthur thought a while and said, "I love Connie. She means everything to me. Yes, I guess I would want her to have the house."

Now I understood where he was coming from, however I was still opposed to putting it in her name. I offered other solutions. "There are several ways that you could buy the house and arrange to have it inherited by Connie once you die, such as owning it jointly, or setting up a trust, or a Life Estate Interest."

"What's a Life Estate interest?"

I explained, "You can buy the house in your name as the owner of a Life Estate. That means you live in the house for the rest of your life. Connie's name goes on the deed as the owner of the Remainder Interest, however she cannot take possession of the house until you die. Once you die, she will own it automatically without the need for probate. This satisfies both your requirements. Connie's name is on the deed, however it's your house for the rest of your life. Once you die she owns it 100% ."

We discussed the other ways to have Connie inherit the home. Arthur liked the Life Estate best. He said he would talk it over with Connie and let me know.

I guess Connie was none too happy with not having the house in her name only because it was several days until I heard from Arthur again, "OK. We're going to do the Life Estate thing. Connie agrees that we don't want to have the investigator bothering us again. He made such a big thing over a car. He would be sure to investigate again if I gave Connie a house."

"I think it very important that we have a clear record that you knew exactly what you were doing when you gave Connie the Remainder Interest in the home. I recommend that we do the closing in my office so that I can videotape the purchase."

And that is what we did. Before closing, I had Arthur videotaped showing that he understood the meaning of a Life Estate. He explained that he was keeping a Life Estate for himself and giving the Remainder Interest to Connie in exchange for all of the care she had been, and would be, giving him.

I also taped the closing. I asked Arthur questions during the closing to show that Arthur knew what he was doing as he purchased the home.

I made sure that Connie was not in the room during the video taping. By taking all of these precautions, I felt confident that if anyone challenged the transaction we could prove that there was no undue influence, and that Arthur had capacity at the time of the purchase, namely that he knew exactly what he was doing when he took title to the house.

I gave the original videotape to Arthur and kept a copy for my file.

After closing I suggested that Arthur do some estate planning, "Do you have a Will?

"No. All my money is in this house. When I die it will go to Connie."

"It could happen that money comes into your Estate, after you die. You could die in a house fire and the fire insurance money be paid to your Estate. Without a Will those insurance funds will go to your next of kin."

"You mean my daughter, Isabella?"

"Yes, she's your only living heir."

"That's all right. She can have it if that happens."

I was also concerned about his care during his life time and tried to explain the importance of a Power of Attorney and a Health Care Directive.

I said, "You know that Parkinson's is a progressive disease. That means it will probably get worse over time. There may come a time when you won't be able to sign your own name. Have you thought of giving someone a Power of Attorney to pay your bills in the event you can't?"

"No. I haven't thought about it. I will, if I see that I'm getting worse."

"Medical decisions are another problem. You might become so ill that you can't talk. Someone will need to make medical decisions for you. Generally doctors turn to the patient's next of kin. In your case, that would be your daughter. If you want Connie to speak for you instead of your daughter, you need to sign a Health Care Directive giving Connie that authority."

He said he would think about it and get back to me. He didn't.

It was more than a year later when I got a call from Connie. She had to place Arthur in a nursing home when his condition become too much for her to handle at home. As soon as his daughter discovered that Arthur was in the nursing home she filed a petition to be appointed as his Guardian.

I went to the nursing home to see what was going on. Arthur was sitting in a wheel chair. He face had a frozen look. It looked like his disease had progressed to the point where he was unable to move or communicate. I spoke to him, but he didn't seem to recognize me. He didn't even respond to Connie when she spoke to him.

No doubt the Court would find him to be in need of a Guardian.

I told Connie that I would file a Notice of Appearance telling the Court that I was Arthur's lawyer and that the judge did not need to appoint any other attorney for him.

Connie asked me, "How can Isabella be his Guardian? I'm the one who has been taking care of him. Not her. I should be Guardian, not her."

I agreed with Connie. I had her return to my office with me to complete an application for Connie to be appointed Guardian. Connie seemed to be having trouble completing the form, "Why do I need to answer all of these questions?"

"Do you have a problem?"

"Yes, I'm not legal." She then told me the story of how she entered this country so many years ago as an illegal alien. "If I fill in these forms, they might find out and send me back to Mexico."

Isabella would be sure to challenge Connie's appointment. It wouldn't take too much effort on her attorney's part to discover that Connie was an illegal alien. This was a major problem. If Isabella became Guardian she would need to file an inventory. She would see the deed with the Remainder Interest to Connie.

I wondered if Arthur's daughter already knew about the house, "Does Isabella know that Arthur bought the house you're in?"

Connie said that Arthur told her that he bought the house in his own name, "He told Isabella that my name was not on the deed."

Lying is always a bad idea. In this case, it could lead to a court battle. Once Isabella saw the deed she might challenge it thinking that her father didn't know what he was doing when he bought the house. The videotape of the transaction would show that Arthur had good reason to put Connie's name on the deed and did so of his own free will. Still, I was concerned about having Isabella as Guardian. That's not what Arthur would want.

I asked Connie to tell me all of the reasons she thought Isabella should not be Guardian. She had a bagful. "Isabella and her father fight all the time. She's always broke and asks him for money. She even lost her home when she didn't pay the mortgage. She got very mad that her father wouldn't make her back payments, He said it was no use because she couldn't afford the house anyway and it wouldn't be long before she would be behind again. She never keeps a job. She always quits or gets fired within a few months. She has a very bad temper and curses at her father all the time . . ."

Only Connie said all this with a rapid-fire Spanish accent, making it hard for me to understand every word — still enough to know that it shouldn't be too hard to have Isabella disqualified as Guardian.

I wondered who to suggest in place of Isabella. Connie was out of the question. Perhaps a professional Guardian? My thoughts turned to my nemesis, Wecco. Who would he be willing to appoint in place of Isabella? Over two years had passed since he was appointed to the Probate Division. I had a lot of opportunity to observe his performance in court. Although he had a reputation for not playing favorites, that was not my experience.

He did not like professional Guardians who did the work for a living. He gave them a hard time even when they came before him with a simple request.

Wecco seemed to like Guardians who did the work for charitable reasons. I thought this understandable because in our county, charitable organizations did most of the guardianships for those developmentally disabled persons without money, property, and no friend or relative willing to serve as Guardian.

I knew that if I asked a charitable organization to serve as Guardian, Judge Wecco would be pleased to throw a plum their way, namely, a Ward with money to pay their Guardian's fee. This would be a way for him to compensate the charitable organization for all of the work they do without pay as Guardian for the poor.

I made an appointment to meet with the administrator in charge of the guardianship program of a charitable organization.

Ms. Perry was a grey-haired lady with a soft voice and placid demeanor. "We'll be happy to help you. We do this all the time. We have a comprehensive guardianship program. We have eleven specially trained geriatric counselors. Each of them is in charge of six or seven wards. We'll take good care of Arthur."

"I didn't know you had such a large guardianship program."

Ms. Perry smiled at me sweetly "Come, I'll give you a tour of our facility."

The guardianship hearing was almost too easy. The judge quickly determined that Arthur was incapacitated and in need of a Guardian. Isabella was there with her attorney asking to be Guardian. Ms. Perry was there with her attorney, asking that the charitable organization be appointed as Guardian.

As Arthur's attorney, I recommended that the charitable organization be appointed. I explained that I did not think Isabella was qualified to be Guardian because she lived so far away and also because of a long history of strained relationship between she and her father. "The most important reason not to appoint the daughter as Guardian, your Honor, is that she is not a financially responsible person. Her credit report shows a foreclosure and a long list of delinquent accounts. May I approach the bench with her credit report?"

There was still that long red line on the floor that Wecco had installed to separate him from the attorneys. I remembered to ask permission to step over the line so that I could give him the report.

I was given permission.

The judge looked at the report, and in the next breath appointed the charitable organization as Arthur's Guardian.

Chapter 5a   The Charitable Guardian

As we left the court room, Ms. Perry and Ed, the attorney for the charitable organization, stopped to speak to Isabella and her attorney out of my earshot. After a few minutes, Isabella was smiling and her attorney was giving Ed his card.

After Isabella left, Ed and Ms. Perry came over and asked me to join them for a cup of coffee. As we sat down, I commented that I thought I knew all of the Elder Law attorneys in our county, yet I didn't remember meeting Ed before.

Ed said, "Probably not. My firm mostly does litigation."

I thought that strange. Why would a charitable organization have a litigator represent them in a guardianship?

I asked Ms. Perry, "I would have thought with all the guardianships you have that you would use an Elder Law attorney to handle these guardianships?"

"We do use Elder Law attorneys. However when there's a paying client we like to use Ed. He's been a big supporter of our charity over the years and its our way of saying 'thank you'."

I had the feeling that I was missing something. I never earned a lot of money working as the attorney for the Guardian. It's mostly administrative work. How could working as lawyer for the Guardian be a pay-back?

Something wasn't adding up.

Ms. Perry wanted to get to the business at hand, namely taking possession of Arthur's property. I told her that I would have Connie collect all his possessions and turn them over to her.

Ed was curious about Connie, "Why didn't she ask to be appointed Guardian?"

"She has two small children. Now that Arthur is in the nursing home, she'll need to find another job. She is a single mom, so it isn't going to be easy for her. I don't think she felt up to taking on this responsibility."

I could see by the way he looked at me that he wasn't buying my story.

He suggested that we all meet with Connie at my office to transfer Arthur's property to the Guardian. I agreed and called Connie to arrange the meeting.

Ms. Perry and Ed were all smiles and charming that day we met with Connie. They asked her how she came to meet Arthur, and how long she had worked for him. And ever so gently Ms. Perry asked, "I heard his daughter asked the Department of Aging to investigate a gift Arthur gave you."

I interrupted, "I represented Arthur during that investigation. I'm sure you have their finding that no exploitation had taken place."

I guessed right because Ed said, "Yes, we have a copy of their report." As I suspected Ed had indeed been in touch with Isabella. For some reason he was trying to find out as much as he could about the relationship between Arthur and Connie.

Connie had all of Arthur's personal effects in a shopping bag. Ed put on a pair of latex gloves and examined each item as she handed it to over to him. Ms. Perry made a written record of the transfer. They were acting as if they were collecting evidence from a crime scene.

"One wristwatch, one wedding ring, one pocket watch, a two dollar bill, a coin collection consisting of pennies, nickels and quarters. "

He asked Connie, "Do you have any idea of the value of his coin collection?

She answered that she had no idea what it was worth. She just brought everything of his that she could find.

When she got to Arthur's business records both Ms. Perry and Ed were full of questions, "I don't see a key to a safe deposit box. Does he have one?"

Connie answered, "No. He doesn't."

"Did he have any CD that was cashed in?"

Now I was getting annoyed. I asked Connie, "Did you bring all of Arthur's business records with you today."

"Yes."

I turned to Ed and said, "Have Ms. Perry make a record of what Connie is giving her, without the cross examination!"

He got the message, but he couldn't contain himself when he saw the deed to house, "A Life Estate? I thought he bought the house in his name only."

I answered, "The closing took place here in my office. I can assure you that Arthur had full capacity at the time. There was absolutely no undue influence. I can and will be happy to produce proof of what I'm saying should there be any question of the transaction."

I moved them to the door and said, "Now that you have all of Arthur's property, I have other clients waiting for me and I 'm sure you are just as busy."

I motioned Connie to stay behind. Once I was sure they had left my office I told Connie, "Do not speak to either of those two unless you have your own attorney present."

She nodded her head in agreement, "Can you be my lawyer?"

"No. Connie, I'm Arthur's lawyer. I suspect things might get nasty down the road. I want to be able to testify about this transfer as his lawyer. If I represent you, it might be considered a conflict of interest."

"What nasty? What could they do?"

I answered, "I don't know. Ed is a litigator. He might want to challenge the validity of the deed in court."

"What does mean?"

"If he can prove that Arthur did not know what he was doing when he purchased the house, he could ask the Court to take your name off of the deed."

Connie couldn't believe this was happening, "Why would he want to do something like that?"

Why indeed? I didn't reply, yet I knew the answer. All the pieces of the puzzle now fit. There's no money in guardianship. There is in litigation. That's what the lawyer for the charitable organization was doing. He was looking for some transfer made by the Ward to challenge in court. It is easy to second guess someone who is incapacitated and unable to speak for himself. Any transfer made by the Ward within a year or two before he is found to be incapacitated can be suspect. Did the Ward actually make a gift, or did the beneficiary of the gift use undue influence on someone with a failing mind?

All the lawyer for the Guardian needed to do was sniff around for the transfer, and then ask the judge to allow him to file a lawsuit to get the property returned to the Ward. The Ward has no say in the matter, still he pays for the lawsuit. The one to profit, besides the lawyer, is whoever inherits the ward's Estate. No wonder Ed was so eager to speak to Isabella at the court house and she very pleased to do so.

Sure enough, within the week I received a copy of petition filed by the Guardian asking the Court to authorize a lawsuit to revoke the gift of the Remainder Interest. The petition alleged that Connie had used fraud, duress and undue influence on a man with diminished capacity.

I called Connie. She was understandably upset. I told her that as Arthur's lawyer I would fight this petition. I had the tape of the closing and I would present it to the judge at the hearing. "Connie, I have to tell you, I've been before this judge many times. There is a good chance he will side with the Guardian. I think you should begin to look for an attorney who is experienced in guardianship litigation."

At the hearing, Ed presented his argument to Judge Wecco, "Your Honor the Ward was ill with Parkinsons when he employed Consuela as his cleaning woman. He was already too disabled to take care of his own home when he met her. In a very short period of time he was paying her much more than the going rate for house cleaning and giving her expensive gifts — including an expensive car. This housekeeper is being investigated because of these transfers. We can show that Consuela used fraud, duress, and undue influence to get the Ward to give her the Remainder Interest in his home. We ask this Court to give us the authority to go forward with this lawsuit."

I presented my argument, "First off, there was an investigate and absolutely no evidence of exploitation was found. The investigation is closed. There is no ongoing investigation. The proposed lawsuit makes no sense. The Ward has a Life Estate interest in this home. Consuela has no right to the property until he dies. If the Guardian were successful in rescinding the Remainder Interest, the only one to profit would be the beneficiary of the Ward's Estate. Why spend the Ward's money on a law suit that doesn't profit him?"

Ed countered, "It may be that the Ward runs out of money and we will need to sell the house to pay for his care."

I argued, "If you spend all of his money on this lawsuit, no doubt he will soon be destitute. However, the Guardian will not prevail in this matter. I have a videotape of the purchase of the house. It clearly shows that the Ward knew exactly what he was doing when he gave his Remainder Interest to Consuela. The gift was in exchange for the care she was giving to him."

"Great," smiled Ed. "Then we have an alternate theory of breach of contract. He's still alive and she's not taking care of him."

I answered, "There's no breach of contract. The Ward needs 24 hour skilled nursing care. Connie doesn't have the nursing skills, or the physical strength to care for him. She's barely 5 foot tall and he's almost 6 foot."

The judge had heard enough. "All of these facts will be for the jury to decide. I am allowing this lawsuit to go forward."

Within the month Ed filed the lawsuit. Connie employed an attorney as soon as I told her how the judge had ruled. She hired Valerie, an experienced litigator, however not in the field of guardianship. Valerie made an appointment with me as soon as Connie was served with the summons.

Valerie told me that she had done quite a bit of trial work in Family Law, "Connie tells me that you taped the closing and that you can prove that Arthur fully understood what he was doing when he gave Connie the Remainder Interest."

"Yes. He had been through one investigation and he wanted to be sure that he would not have a problem in the future. I not only taped him during the closing, I taped an interview with him before the closing where he explains his understanding of a Life Estate interest, and why he decided to give Connie the Remainder Interest. "

I showed the tapes to Valerie. She said, "Now I know why Ed alleged an alternative count in the lawsuit for breach of contract. The interview seems to imply that the gift was contingent on Connie taking care of Arthur until he died."

I said I didn't think that count would hold up, "Arthur and I spoke about what would happen if Connie could no longer care for him. Arthur told me that he wanted her to have the house regardless of whether she actually took care of him. He knew that he might become so ill so as to make it impossible for Connie to continue with his care."

Valerie agreed, "Connie tells me that Arthur is six foot tall. She's just five foot. There is no way she can take care of him in his current condition. You can't have breach of contract, if it is impossible to perform the contract. I don't understand. From reading his medical records showing that Arthur needs 24 hour skilled nursing care and looking at the tape of the closing, they can't win."

I explained, "It doesn't matter. Win or lose, Ed gets paid, and that's all he's interested in."

"We have laws that punish the plaintiff for filing a frivolous lawsuit. I can get him to pay for my attorney fees."

"I don't think you'll be successful getting a judge to agree that this is a frivolous lawsuit. The Guardian will say that she was only following the judge's order to proceed with the lawsuit. Whoever the judge is in civil court to hear the case is not about to override the ruling of a judge in Probate Court. Even if the civil judge determined that this is a frivolous lawsuit, once the probate judge makes an order, the Guardian is released from all liability."

Valerie gave a long low whistle when the full impact of what was going on in the guardianship court hit her. "This is legalized corruption. There should be strict guide lines that a judge should be required to follow before allowing a Guardian to start a lawsuit."

"There aren't any such guide lines right now."

Valerie wondered "You'd think the judge would notice a pattern when certain Guardians keep coming before him asking to sue on behalf of the Ward?

"Yes, you'd think."

Regardless of what Valerie and I thought of the merits of the case, it went forward. Within a few months Ed scheduled my deposition and Connie's deposition to be taken at Ed's office. My deposition was to be held first. Connie came early and was waiting in the reception area. My deposition was surprisingly short. Ed only asked me a few questions and then asked Connie to come into the conference room.

We were startled by the appearance of police officers and immigration authorities. The officer said that Connie was an illegal alien and that they were deporting her back to Mexico. Connie burst into tears. Her legs buckled beneath her. Luckily, Valerie was there for Connie and she accompanied her to immigration headquarters.

Once they left I turned on Ed, "You planned all this! Now I know why you took Arthur's property with latex gloves. You wanted to be sure you had Connie's fingerprints."

He said with a righteous air, "I suspected she was hiding a criminal background. I didn't know she was an illegal immigrant. Once I found out that who she was, it was my duty as an American citizen and as an officer of the court to notify Immigration."

There were things I wanted to say like, "How do you sleep nights?" or "You make me sick" or "You are evil personified."

However as I looked at his smug expression, I realized he scheduled my deposition so that I would be present when Connie was arrested. Seeing my anger is exactly what he wanted. No. I wouldn't give him that satisfaction. Instead I said, "I know what you're doing and no doubt have done in many other cases. Eventually, everyone else will figure it out. You can't hide under the robes of the Court forever," and I walked out of the room.

Connie was deported back to Mexico. She choose to have her children remain with their father until she could appeal the ruling and return to this country legally.

A few months later I received a call from Mexico. It was Connie. She said that Ed offered to settle the case, "Valerie says that without me being there to testify, it will be hard to win. Ed offered enough for me to pay Valerie with $10,000 left over for me."

"And you won't have any more right to inherit the house?"

"Yes. I have to give up all my rights to the house."

"Connie, you need to make your own decision about whether you want to settle. The only thing I can suggest is that you ask an accountant evaluate your Remainder Interest. There are Life Estate tables based on the life expectancy of the owner of the Life Estate. The accountant will take the current market value of the house and multiply it by a percentage based on Arthur's life expectancy. He will subtract the value of Arthur's Life Estate interest from the market value of the house. Whatever is left is equal to the value of your Remainder Interest. If that value is higher than what Ed is offering, you may want to have Valerie negotiate for a better deal."

I don't know exactly how the case turned out because Ed moved to have me dismissed as Arthur's lawyer saying there was no further need for my services, and of course Wecco granted the petition.

Some months later, I met Valerie at one of our Bar luncheons. She gave me an update on her client, "Connie is still in Mexico. She hired an immigration attorney to get permission to return to the United States. He said she has a good chance of success, based on the fact that her husband and children are American citizens."

Valerie went on to say that they settled the case. She didn't say for how much, yet she seemed satisfied with the settlement. I wondered if Connie was equally as pleased.

Valerie said that when they went before the judge to have the settlement approved, he also authorized the Guardian to sell the house to pay for the litigation.

I asked, "So the Guardian used Arthur's money to fight the case as plaintiff, and then the Guardian used Arthur's money to pay the defendant to settle the case?"

"That's right."

"And the house Arthur wanted Connie to have had to be sold to pay for all this?"

"Yup."

"It's a good thing Arthur is too sick to know what's going on."

Valerie agreed "That's for sure."

The Developmentally Disabled 6

Janet came out of the shower laughing, "This change of life is kicking."

Her husband, Ken, asked, "What are you talking about?"

"Remember when I went to the doctor a few months ago? I was there for a cold. When I mentioned that I skipped a period, he said I was probably beginning my change. This is no change, I'm pregnant!"

Ken was incredulous, "That can't be. We've been having sex all our married lives without birth control. How can you be having a baby now? It took you forever to get pregnant with Vickie. You had to take all those fertility shots and more to stay pregnant. It was the same with Ellen. Even with all those treatments, it took over a year to get pregnant. Ellen was harder than Vickie. You had to stay in bed for almost the whole pregnancy. How could you possibly get pregnant — and stay pregnant — without going through fertility treatments? No. It must be gas."

He looked at her and said, "Besides you don't look pregnant."

Janet laughed, "At my weight the kid would have to be pretty darned big before he shows himself behind my fat belly. I know a kick when I feel it. This isn't the change of life and it's not gas. It's a baby. I don't know how it happened." She smiled and said "I guess we'll just have to name it Miracle."

Ken was not smiling. In fact, he was very angry, "You're not seriously considering having a child? I'm 52. You're 43. I'm not going to raise kids when I'm an old man. No. You'll have to get an abortion."

His response shocked Janet, "This is a child. Your child. A real person. It's kicking. You're not saying get an abortion. You're saying kill a baby. Your baby. What's the matter with you anyway?"

The argument continued well into the night. Ken gave reason after reason to not have the child. Ken did have one concern that Janet shared as well. It was Down Syndrome. He said, "At our age there's a good chance that this child will have Down Syndrome. I tell you, Jan, raising kids is hard enough. I know I can't raise a disabled child. I just can't."

Jan said, "I did read somewhere that having a child with Down was more likely for older parents. I'll schedule an amniocentesis to see if it is a Down baby. I'll also have a sonogram to be sure the baby's healthy.

Ken said, "And if it has Down, you promise to abort?"

"I promise nothing. This is a human being. A child. Our child. I won't commit murder."

As it was, the tests turned out just fine. The sonogram showed they were having a boy. Janet was overjoyed that she was having a son.

Ken still didn't want the child.

His next argument was that of adoption, "We have two girls. That's enough. We don't need any more children. You forget how much work it is. Forget about sleep for at least a year. I'll be 53 when he's born. We know he's a healthy baby. Why don't you do something generous in your life and give this baby to a couple who can't have children?"

Janet made her position clear, "This child is a blessing — my blessing. I am not giving him up for adoption."

Arguments over the pregnancy did not go unnoticed by the couple's daughters. Victoria at 11 didn't know what to make of the imminent birth. She told her friends about the baby and was warned that she would soon become a baby sitter, changing diapers and cleaning up puke. Ellen at 8 was daddy's girl. Her friends told her that she wouldn't be the baby of the family any more. She would have to share her parent's affection with a baby brother. Ellen didn't worry about dad liking her brother more than her. From the way he talked, he didn't want anything to do with the child.

The baby was born prematurely on December 25th. He was transferred to the neonatal unit. It was almost a month before he was allowed to go home. Doctors assured the couple that the baby would be just fine.

Janet insisted that the baby be named after his father. She told Ken, "He looks just like you. We should name him Kenneth. He'll be Ken, Jr." Ken knew that his wife was just trying to make him bond with his son. Still, the baby was cute and he was his son, so he agreed to the name.

Kenneth kept his distance from the baby during the year following the birth. Janet wanted this kid. Let her take care of it. As Kenny got to be a toddler, Janet tried to get Kenneth to hold his child. The baby looked away and squirmed out of his hands. Janet accused Ken of not loving his child, "You never look at him. What kind of father are you?"

Kenneth was defensive, "I try to look at him, but he never looks back at me. He never looks at anyone."

Janet said, "Sure he does." She picked him up and tried to get him to look in her eyes. He turned his head and tried to get back down to the floor. Janet persisted. That only set Kenny off into a temper tantrum.

Besides avoiding eye contact, Kenny didn't like to be touched. Janet noticed that he wasn't as cuddly as his sisters, however she attributed this to the fact that he was a boy. Whenever she took him to the pediatrician, the doctor said his rate of growth and development were perfect for his age.

By the time Kenny was three, Janet began to worry that something was wrong. He seemed overly shy. When she took him to the playground, he wouldn't play with the other children. He'd look at them from a safe distance. He didn't like outdoor noises. If a loud truck drove by, he'd look worried. A barking dog or a passing fire engine would set him off crying. He was difficult to manage even when he was home. Anything could provoke a temper tantrum. Sometimes he would cry and scream for no reason at all.

When she told the pediatrician about Kenny's reaction to dogs, trucks, noises in general, and the fact that he didn't play with other children, the doctor said "He's just a timid child. He'll outgrow it."

He didn't. Things just got worse. Instead of adding words to his vocabulary, he seemed to forget the words he knew. His tantrums became a daily occurrence. He would get so angry, he would bang his head against anything that happened to be near him — couch, chair, wall.

The pediatrician wasn't concerned. He said that Kenny was just one of many children who were difficult to raise. This was the 1970s and doctors at that time weren't as alert to developmental disorders as they would later become.

Janet couldn't talk to her husband about the problem. He never had any patience with the child. Ken spent more and more time at work. He always seemed to be going on a business trip, leaving Janet with the growing burden of raising a difficult boy and two teenage daughters.

Just before his fifth birthday, Kenny threw a temper tantrum and from there went into a seizure. Janet rushed him to the hospital. After a battery of tests and an evaluation by a neurologist, the diagnosis was grim. Kenny did indeed have developmental disorders. His doctor thought he might have autism. He also had neurological problems. His brain was misfiring. He had epilepsy.

Instead of being supportive to Janet, or concerned about his son, Ken worried about his own future "Why did I work so hard all my life? So that I could spend my old age taking care of a retard? I told you I didn't want this child. I knew this would happen."

He mocked Janet, "Your gift from heaven. He's a gift from hell! He'll never get better. He'll never grow up. You can spend the rest of your life taking care of a two year old. I won't!"

With that Ken packed his bags and moved out of the house. Within the week, Ken made an appointment with his lawyer. He began the visit with a discussion of his son and how he wanted no part of raising the child. The attorney said, "It seems to me that what you really want is to terminate your parental rights."

"I don't want to terminate all of my parental rights. I just don't want to be responsible for my son's care. Raising a disable child is a never ending job. I don't want Janet coming to me when it gets too much for her to handle and telling me to take care of him." Ken said emphatically, "I won't let that happen."

"How does your wife feel about this?"

Ken said, "I don't know. I haven't spoken to her since he was diagnosed."

The lawyer advised, "Either you need to talk to her, or she needs to get an attorney who I can talk to. Regardless of whether you two come to an agreement as to your custodial duties, the Court will not allow her to be solely responsible for his support. In fact, when the judge hears that this boy is disabled, and you want her to raise him by herself, he will probably make you responsible for her support and for the support of your child."

Ken was not dissuaded, "I don't care. I just want out."

Janet and Ken never did speak to each other. Their lawyers worked out a settlement. Jan was given sole custody of the children. Ken was required to pay alimony to Jan for fifteen years, set up a lifetime trust for his son and pay all of the legal costs of the divorce, including Janet's attorney fees.

The lawyers had Ken employ an attorney, who specialized in trust design, to create a trust to meet Kenny's special needs. The trust took into account the possibility of qualifying for Medicaid or other medical assistance from state, federal government or charitable sources. It made funds available to provide Kenny with some quality of life, such as clothing, toys, or special educational outings. Money from the trust was to be paid to the person or agency who had legal responsibility for Kenny's custodial care.

The divorce itself took less than fifteen minutes. The judge approved the settlement and announced to the couple "You are now freed from the bonds of matrimony."

Ken muttered under his breath, "And from the bonds of paternity."

That first year after the divorce was the hardest year of Janet's life. Although Ken had spent little time at home in the past few years, she still missed him. They had a long history together. She spent half her life with him. Now he was gone, and she felt empty.

The children were almost more than she could handle. Kenny was a 24 hour job. The girls were no help even though Vickie was 17 and Ellen 14. The divorce left them angry and sad. They blamed their brother for the loss of their father. They refused to assist with Kenny's care.

Kenneth didn't ask to have his parental rights with his daughters terminated, yet for all intents and purposes, he terminated those rights as well. He took a job in another state. He would call on occasion, birthdays, holidays, graduation, however, he didn't ask either of his daughters to come and visit with him, and he never came to see them.

The girls felt abandoned. Especially Ellen. Her father always told her she was Daddy's little princess. What did she do to make him reject her? Vickie knew she was not her father's favorite, however if she had a choice she would have gone with him. Instead, she was stuck in a house with a screaming brother and a tearful mother. Yes, that first year was hard on everyone.

Jan couldn't say exactly when things began to change. Kenny was put on medication that controlled the intensity and frequency of his seizures. She enrolled him in a special school for the developmentally disabled. He made his first friend at that school. He learned to express what he wanted instead of throwing temper tantrums. He began to smile. Jan hadn't seen him smile that way since he was a baby. Tears of joy rolled down her face, the first time he hugged her and said, "Mommy love."

There were still the hard days, yet every advance Kenny made no matter how small, was a reason to celebrate. As much heartache as Kenny caused, that's how much happiness he brought into her life. Kenny and his disabilities became the focus of Janet's life. She joined support groups. She shared experiences with other parents of disabled children. She became an advocate for the rights of disabled children. She organized fund raising events for autism research. Kenny gave her life meaning and purpose.

Least you think this story has a happy ending. It doesn't.

Kenny did make progress, however there seemed to be an invisible ceiling beyond which he could not go. Yes, he could walk and talk, but he could not read. He could recite the alphabet and count to ten, yet there was no indication that he knew what he was saying. It was just repetitive behavior, and Kenny was good at that. He would take some word or phrase and repeat and repeat it for days on end, until another word or phrase took his fancy.

The attention Janet gave to Kenny was hard for Vickie and Ellen to accept. Sure Mom was pleased when they did something good like getting an "A" in English, however she expected such things from them. Not so with Kenny. Anything new that <u>he</u> was able to master was met with joy and great fanfare.

Both girls left the house at their first opportunity. Vickie went off to college. Ellen went to work after high school and married the next year. Janet was sad to see them go, yet happy that they had no developmental problems. She was relieved that they had grown into normal adults and were off on their own.

Janet was content to live with and care for Kenny. As she aged, she began to think about what would happen to Kenny after she died. She didn't dwell on it it. She knew that the trust fund was there for Kenny's support and he had two sisters who would look out for him.

It was a family tradition to get together and celebrate the holidays and Kenny's birthday all at the same time. Janet planned weeks in advance for Kenny's 25th birthday. Ellen's twin boys were 10 years old. Kenny looked forward to their visit. He never grew past five feet. He was always on the slight side. At 25, he was still a little boy who enjoyed playing with his cousins.

Kenny didn't interact with Vickie. He kept his distance from her. Jan thought it might be because Vickie had no children of her own. Vickie quit college to marry. That didn't last long. Then again, continuity was never her thing. Vickie never stayed in one place or job for long. She hopscotched all over the United States. Jan didn't understand Victoria's life style. Yet Vickie seemed happy, and that was good enough for Janet.

Janet enjoyed the visit with the family, however all of the cooking and cleaning left her exhausted. She thought it was her age. After all, she was almost 70.

When the girls left Jan said to Kenny, "It was nice to have the family together for the holidays, but its good to see them all go home." Jan laughed, and Kenny laughed too. He didn't fully grasp what she was saying, still anytime Mom laughed was a good reason to laugh too.

The next morning Kenny came down for his breakfast. Mom seemed to be sleeping on the floor. He pushed her to wake her. She didn't move. He started to scream at her to wake up. She still didn't move. Kenny began to panic. He saw the next door neighbor leaving his house to go to work. He ran outside and pulled the neighbor's arm to come into his house.

After that things got very confusing for Kenny. An ambulance came to his house with waves of siren sounds. Kenny reverted back to the days when the sound of an ambulance was more than he could handle. He cried and screamed. The police placed him with the Department of Health Services until they were able to contact family members.

Kenny didn't understand the funeral services. He cried for his mother. Ellen said Mom was in heaven. That only confused him. He wanted her here. Not some other place. Victoria said to Ellen, "Maybe we should have allowed him to come to the wake, so he could see that she's dead."

Ellen didn't think that would have helped, "She was dead when he found her. He told the neighbor that she was sleeping on the floor. I think he'll eventually figure out that she's not coming back."

After the funeral, Vickie said, "I'm going to stay here at the house and take care of Kenny."

Ellen was surprised. She never saw any affection between Vickie and Kenny. She never knew Vickie to voluntarily assume any responsibility. Still if that's what Vickie wanted, it would take the problem of Kenny's care off of Ellen's shoulders for the time being. Ellen offered to have Kenny stay at her house whenever Vickie needed a break.

The conversation turned to their inheritance. Ellen said, "All that Mom had was this house and a bank account. She put my name on the account in case of emergency. She had a Will leaving everything to us. She didn't leave anything to Kenny because he has his own trust account."

Vickie asked, "How did she take money out of the trust account?"

Ellen said "She just went to the trust company. It's over on 10th Street. She would just go in, sign a statement saying what the money was for, and they would write out a check. If we need money for Kenny, we can get it from the trust officer."

Vickie changed the subject, "What are we going to do with the house?"

"I guess the first thing is to go see a lawyer with Mom's Will. He'll get the house transferred to our names. That will probably take a few months. After that, we'll decide if we want to sell it. If you're living with Kenny in the house we may want to just leave it in both our names."

The girls employed an attorney to probate their mother's estate. He said they could serve together as Co-Personal Representatives. Ellen withdrew the money from the joint bank account. She set aside enough money to pay for the probate and split the rest with Vickie.

After Ellen went home, Victoria went straight to the trust company and tried to make a withdrawal. The trust officer said that only Kenny's legal Guardian could make a withdrawal. He explained that she would need to go to a lawyer who would put in a petition to have her appointed as Kenny's Guardian.

Victoria went back to the lawyer and asked him to get her appointed as Guardian. He explained, "A limited guardianship can be established for a developmentally disabled adult. The Court will limit the powers given to the Guardian to only those things the Ward is unable to do for himself. The goal is to allow a Ward who is developmentally disabled to be as self sufficient as possible."

"You don't have to worry about Kenny doing anything for himself. He has the I.Q. of a two year old."

Something about the tone of Victoria's voice as she spoke of Kenny made the attorney wary. "Did you discuss this guardianship with your sister?"

"We agreed that I would take care of Kenny."

"But did you discuss becoming his Guardian?"

"No. This just came up because of Kenny's trust account. We needed money to take care of Kenny. The trust officer said we can't withdraw money for Kenny unless someone is his Guardian."

The lawyer was concerned about a conflict of interest, "You and your sister employed me to probate your mother's Estate. I can represent you in your brother's guardianship if your sister consents, in writing, to your appointment as Guardian. If not, I can't represent either of you. I have a form that Ellen can sign waiving (giving up) her right to serve as Guardian and agreeing to your appointment. I'll put it in the mail to her. If she signs it, we can go forward with the guardianship."

Once she left the office, Vickie thought she better call Ellen before the lawyer's letter had a chance to arrive.

Ellen's response was explosive. "Now I know why you want to take care of Kenny. You want to get to the money in the trust fund. You haven't changed. You're just the same greedy pig you always were. No. I won't sign any paper. In fact, I'm going to call the lawyer and tell him I want to be Guardian!"

The lawyer told Ellen the same as he told Vickie, "I can't represent one of my clients against another of my clients. That's a conflict of interest. I can still be your lawyer and Vickie's lawyer in the probate – provided you don't have some quarrel over the probate. You'll each need to employ your own attorney when it comes to being appointed as Kenny's Guardian."

And that's what they each did.

In most guardianship matters, an attorney is appointed by the Court to represent the incapacitated person. The attorney is chosen by the Clerk of the court on a rotation basis. Lawyers volunteer to serve as a court appointed attorney as needed. The Clerk puts the lawyer's name on a list and then calls lawyers in the order as their names appear on the list. I guess my name was next because I got a call from the Clerk asking whether I could serve as the lawyer for a man with developmental disabilities. The case sounded interesting, so I agreed to take it.

As the court appointed attorney of a developmentally disabled person, I needed to determine whether a guardianship was in his best interest, and if so, what type of guardianship (person, or property, or both) would be appropriate.

The first thing I did was go to the courthouse and look at the documents that had been filed in this case. After looking at Kenny's medical record, I knew that a full guardianship was appropriate. He needed a Guardian to make his medical decisions and take care of his personal needs. He needed a Guardian of his property to use his income from Social Security for his support and to withdraw money from the trust for his special needs.

I visited the trust company to learn more about the terms of the trust. I was referred to the trust officer, Doris Bradley. As two female lawyers, we chatted about our respective practices. Doris was a mother of two young children. She gave up private practice to work full time for the trust company. She told me, "This is a lot easier than private practice. I put in my 9 to 5. I get paid vacations and don't have to worry about lining up other attorney's to take care of my clients while I'm away. Best of all, I get a steady salary and don't have to worry about where the next client is coming from."

I agreed. "People think lawyering is a glamorous business. What they don't know is that it is a lot of hard work and responsibility."

Doris was very helpful. She gave me a copy of the trust in my capacity as attorney for the beneficiary of the trust, namely Kenneth. We exchanged cards. She said to call, if I had any question.

My next job as court appointed attorney, was to determine which of his sisters Kenneth wanted to serve as his Guardian. I needed to meet with him to see whether he preferred one sister over the other. If he had no preference, or if he was too disabled to express his preference, I would need to recommend the sister who, in my opinion, would do the best job of caring for him.

I needed to meet with Kenneth and his two sisters before I could make any recommendation. I called the attorneys who represented the sisters to arrange a meeting. Ellen had employed Keith Hendrick, an attorney new to the practice of law. Vickie employed Mark Grindell.

Because I knew Mark from the Edeeshia Hooper case, I called him first, "Roles are reversed, Mark. You were the court appointed attorney when I was trying to get Edeeshia appointed Guardian. Now I'm the court appointed attorney and you represent Victoria who wants to be Guardian."

Mark said, "I hope you're nicer to me than I was to you."

"No way. I have a reputation to uphold."

He asked "And what reputation is that?"

"No Mercy Pohl."

Mark chuckled, "Right."

Getting to the business at hand, I said, "I'm looking at your client's application. It doesn't tell much about her."

Mark said, "I just met Victoria, so I only know what she put on her application."

"I notice that Kenneth is living with Victoria. I would like to see how they interact with each other within the setting of their home. Can you meet with me at the house?"

"Sure, I'll call Victoria and set up a meeting for tomorrow afternoon."

I was expecting a 25 year old man, so seeing Kenneth for the first time was a surprise. He looked like a teenager and acted like a two year old. He was sitting in a corner of the living room, rocking back and forth, humming to himself.

He didn't seem to be aware that anyone else was in the room. Victoria went over to him and said, "Kenny, honey, we have company. How about saying 'Hello?" He continued to rock and hum.

I knew from the court file that there was nothing wrong with Kenny's hearing, and that he was able to walk and talk. I said to Victoria, "I am Kenny's court appointed attorney, so I would like speak with him in private."

She sniffed, "Good Luck" and left the room with Mark.

Once alone with Kenneth, I sat down quietly beside him. After a few minutes of humming and rocking, he glanced at me then quickly looked away. I told him who I was and that the judge asked me to find out where he wanted to live. "Do you want to live with Ellen or do you want to live with Victoria?"

He resumed his humming and rocking. He wouldn't look at me again. I continued to speak to him, "I hear you have twin cousins. They must be a lot of fun to play with. Do you think you might want to live with them? I want you to be happy wherever you are and I need your help to pick the right home for you. I tell you what I'm going to do. I am giving you this card. Here I'm putting it on your lap. It has my name and phone number on it. You give this card to Victoria if ever you want to talk to me."

I then called in Mark and Victoria. She said in a taunting voice, "You two have a nice chat?"

I answered, "I can't tell you what we spoke about. Attorney client privilege, you know."

For some reason, Victoria looked worried.

I spent the rest of the visit interviewing Victoria, "How long have you been living here with Kenneth?"

"Ever since the funeral. It was my mother's house. Ellen and I inherited it, so I own half."

"Where did you live before here?"

She answered, "I had a studio apartment in Miami. As soon as I heard that Mom died, I gave it up and moved into this house to take care of Kenny."

"Didn't you have a lease?"

"No. I was just renting month to month."

I wondered "Did you give up your job in Miami?"

"No. I was kind of between jobs."

I asked, "What was your last job?"

"I was a sales rep at a sports goods store."

"What store was that?"

Victoria didn't identify the store, "You wouldn't know it. They don't have any stores in this state. They only have one store in Miami."

I asked, "How long did you work as a sales clerk?"

"Over a year, I think. I don't recall the exact date."

Marc was getting increasingly uncomfortable, "Listen Amy, I have to get back to my office. Maybe we could continue this again another day."

I agreed and we parted for the day.

My interview with Ellen was nothing like that Victoria's — starting with the response of her attorney, Keith Hendrick. He didn't feel the need to be present when I interviewed his client. He said, "I'll set up an appointment for you. She's a real fine lady. I know you'll be impressed with her."

And I was.

Ellen was as open as Victoria was evasive. She had been married twelve years. He husband earned a good salary, so she was able to stay home and care for the twins. The only thing she didn't seem to want to talk about was Victoria. I tried an indirect approach, "Why do you think you'd make a better Guardian than Victoria?"

"I'm a mother. I know how to take care of children. Kenny may be 25, but mentally, he's just a child."

I said, "You have more responsibilities than your sister with your own children and husband. Wouldn't she have more time to spend with Kenneth?"

"I'm more settled than Vickie. She's always moving from place to place."

I looked at her and asked pointedly, "Is that the only reason you think Victoria's shouldn't be Kenny's Guardian?"

"No," she said and quickly dropped her eyes.

I persisted, "I need some reason to recommend you over Victoria. Is there anything else you can tell me?"

"I can't think of anything," she said, still avoiding my gaze.

I turned in my report based on the interviews I had conducted. I recommended Ellen. The only reasons I could give were her experience as a mother, the fact that she always lived within driving distance of her mother and that she had much more contact with her brother over the years.

The reports from the Court Investigator did not make a recommendation as to choice of Guardian. However, she said that she did not think Kenneth living at home with Victoria was in his best interest. She believed that he was regressing and needed more stimulation. She recommended that Kenneth be placed in a group home that offered 24 hour supervision and a structured learning program.

I did not look forward to the hearing before Judge Wecco. I had strong feelings about this case, yet nothing concrete to base it on.

Mark's cross examination of Ellen was intense, "If you did not think your sister would be capable of taking care of Kenneth, why did you agree to let her stay in your mother's home and take care of him?"

"I had to go home to take care of the twins. I didn't know she was going to try to make the living arrangement permanent. I thought we were going take care of him together."

Mark persisted, "Did you tell your sister that you expected to share custody?"

"I thought I did. I thought she understood that."

It continued in this manner for over an hour.

Keith, being new to the practice of guardianship, was no match for Mark. His cross examination of Victoria was very weak. It did not address the concerns I had, namely, why she wanted to be Kenny's Guardian. She never showed any interest in him before. And why was it that she never held a steady job and kept moving from place to place?

Keith should have put her in a verbal corner and forced disclosures. He didn't.

I wanted a shot at trying to expose whatever secret she was hiding, "Your Honor, as court appointed attorney for the incapacitated, I ask to be allowed to cross examine this witness."

"Court appointed attorney? I thought I appointed you Guardian Ad Litem," he said as he shuffled through the papers in front of him.

A Guardian Ad Litem is usually appointed for a minor child. The job of the Guardian Ad Litem is to represent the best interests of the minor in whatever hearing is being held before the Court. The main function of the Guardian Ad Litem is to make reports that assist the Court in deciding whatever matter is being decided. It is generally not the job of a Guardian Ad Litem to cross examine witnesses.

"No, your Honor. I was appointed as an attorney. Kenneth is not a child. He is a developmentally disabled adult."

Judge Wecco replied, "I should have appointed you as Guardian Ad Litem. He may be an adult chronologically, but not developmentally. I read your report, Mrs. Pohl. I am well aware that you favor his sister Ellen as Guardian. However, I find Victoria to be better qualified. There is no reason for further cross examination."

And with that he banged his gavel and left the bench.

Chapter 6a   Guardian Devil

Several month passed. I had long since been discharged as Kenny's court appointed attorney. Once I put a case into my closed file, the matter goes out of my head. I had to search my memory bank when I got a call from Doris Bradley, "You remember me. The trust officer of Kenneth's trust."

"Oh yes, yes. How have you been?"

"Fine, but I'm having a problem with his trust account and I was wondering if you could come to my office so I could show the file to you."

I went to Doris' office the next day. When I looked at the trust account records, I could see the reason for Doris' concern. Victoria was making almost daily withdrawals. Checks were made out to her as her brother's Guardian. She would always cash the check before leaving the trust company.

The amounts being withdrawn were getting larger and larger. The reasons for the withdrawal, increasingly contrived — outings for Kenneth, clothes for Kenneth, toys for Kenneth, toiletries for Kenneth, clothes for Kenneth . . .

I promised Doris that I would look into the matter and get back to her. Meanwhile, I asked her to call Victoria and ask her for an accounting of monies spent.

"OK. I'll tell Victoria that we are doing an audit of the account and need receipts for the money she's spent. I'll tell her that we can't allow further withdrawals until we have a full accounting."

I drove directly to the house. It looked so different from my last visit that I thought I had the wrong place. The grass needed cutting. There were newspapers piled up at the door. The plants looked like they hadn't been watered. Many of them were dead or dying.

I knocked on the door and rang the door bell. No one answered. Her car was in the driveway so I knew Victoria was home. I kept ringing the doorbell. When I heard Kenny crying inside, I started pounding on the door. Victoria finally opened the door — just a crack. "Wud you want?"

Through the crack I could see that she disheveled and high on something, "I want to see Kenny."

She slurred her words as she said, "No. I saw the order. You're not his lawyer anymore. I don't have to let you in." She shut the door. I heard her yell at Kenny, "Shut up!"

As soon as I got back to my office I called the Department of Health Services and told them that I believed that a developmentally disabled adult was being abused. I gave them Victoria's name and address. They promised to send someone out within 24 hours.

I then called Ellen and told her what I saw, "Why didn't you tell me that Victoria was on drugs? We could have stopped her from being appointed as Kenny's Guardian."

"I suspected, but I didn't know for sure that she was on drugs. We never lived together after she left for college. I never saw her take any drugs when she was living at home. I thought she drank a lot when we got together for the holidays. I saw her drinking — nothing else."

With that Ellen began to cry, "We were never really close as sisters. I didn't know what she was doing. I couldn't accuse her of being an addict when I didn't know for sure."

The next day, I got a call from a case worker who was sent out to investigate. She said, "We found your card in Kenny's room. Are you related to him?"

"No, I'm his court appointed attorney. I can give you the address and telephone number of his sister, Ellen."

She told me that the door was unlocked when she arrived. Kenny was there by himself. It looked like Victoria left the house in a hurry, taking just a few of her belongings.

I realized that Ellen must have called her sister after she spoke to me and warned her about the investigation.

I could hear the anger in the case worker's voice as she described what she found, "This place is filthy. This poor child has open sores and bruises on his body. He looks as if he hasn't been fed or washed in weeks. This is a case of criminal neglect if I ever saw one. I'm filing a police report. I'm taking him to the hospital for treatment. They'll take pictures of him that we can use as evidence."

As soon as I received a copy of the case worker's report, I filed a motion to have Victoria removed based on misconduct in her role as Guardian. I sent a copy of the motion to Ellen's attorney. Ellen still wanted to be Kenny's Guardian, so she had her attorney put in a petition for her to be appointed as successor Guardian.

The Clerk set a hearing for my motion to discharge Victoria as Guardian. Ellen's petition was set for the same hearing.

Judge Wecco quickly approved my motion and removed Victoria as Guardian. His ruling made it clear that she was not being released her from her liability to the Ward. He held her personally liable for the money she removed from Kenneth's trust account plus the loss of interest on that money, plus the costs of bringing this motion before the Court, including my attorney fees.

However Victoria was long since gone. Unless she later got picked up on drug or other criminal charges, I doubted whether she would ever face the criminal charges that were lodged against her for abusing and neglecting Kenny, or that she would ever reimburse his guardian-ship account for the money she was ordered to pay by the Court.

Judge Wecco denied Ellen's request to be Guardian saying, "You never once visited your brother in all the months that your sister was Guardian. Had you cared enough to visit, you might have saved that poor man a lot of suffering. No. I'm appointing Nancy Williams to serve as his Guardian. I am also ordering that Kenneth be placed in the group home recommended by the Court Investigator when we established this guardianship."

Nancy Williams was a professional Guardian. She was well respected in the guardianship community. I worked with her on other cases. I knew she would do a good, conscientious job.

For once I agreed with Judge Wecco's ruling.

The Motherless Child 7

"Beware the good child." Lorraine recalled her mother's warning. Lorraine heard these words when her daughter, Cathy, was about to go to school for the first time. Lorraine was telling her mother how much she enjoyed being with Cathy — how good and sweet the child was — never a bit of trouble. "I'll miss being with her all day."

Lorraine couldn't imagine why her mother would say such a thing, "What does that mean?" Her mother just shrugged her shoulders and the subject was dropped.

It wasn't till many years later when Lorraine began to understand what her mother was saying. Cathy married when she was twenty. Her husband was verbally abusive. He criticized everything Cathy did, everything she said. And she took the criticism, without complaining, as if she deserved it. Luckily, the marriage didn't last very long. He divorced her within the year. Cathy was crushed. She never saw it coming. She tried to do everything right. How could things go so wrong?

Lorraine was overjoyed that Cathy was out of an abusive relationship, however that happiness was short lived. Cathy met and married Jim within a year of her divorce.

In the beginning, Jim and Cathy seemed compatible. They both wanted children, so she had Tammy within a year of their marriage. A month later, Jim insisted that Cathy go back to her waitress job, and she did.

Lorraine was very upset and let Cathy know about it, "You just had a C Section. You're still recuperating. Why isn't he going out to work?"

"You know Jim is a drummer. He takes every local job he can. But the good money is going on the road, and he doesn't want to leave me and the baby alone."

Lorraine continued arguing, "There's other jobs. The guy's a lazy bum. He sits around the house all day drinking beer and playing with his computer while you work your ass off. And why is he always on the Internet? What's he looking for? Pornography?"

Cathy paid no attention to her mother's criticism. Jim told Cathy that he was using the computer to find work and keep up with the latest trends in music, and she believed him.

Even though this was far from a perfect marriage, Cathy was determined to make it work. The pain of her divorce to her first husband was imbedded in her mind. No. She would put up with anything to keep this marriage together, especially now that they were parents.

As time went by Jim became just as verbally abusive as her first husband. He took every opportunity to put Cathy down. He told her that she was lucky that he had married her considering she was had already had one failed marriage. He made her feel like damaged goods.

He criticized everything she did. He made fun of her physical appearance. He "kidded" her about a roll of fat that remained around her middle after her pregnancy.

He told her that she didn't know how to manage money, so he made her give him everything she earned.

As with any abuser, he sought to have total control over her. He set about isolating Cathy so no one could bring to her attention how outrageous his behavior was. He objected to her mother's visits saying that she just came to see what things she could use to criticize him. He told Cathy that her mother was trying to break them up. That's the same thing Cathy's first husband said about her mother. Instead of noticing the same pattern of control and isolation, Cathy sided with Jim and discouraged her mother from visiting. Gradually Cathy retreated into her shell and told her mother nothing more about the way Jim was treating her.

Actually, Cathy didn't need to worry that her mother was trying to break up their marriage. Lorraine accepted the relationship. She finally understood her mother's warning of "Beware the good child." The good child is too obedient. When grown, the good child seeks out a relationship with someone who will tell her what to do. Unfortunately, men who relish such control generally have other personality flaws. The result an abusive relationship or the "Stepford Wife" syndrome — or both.

Lorraine did not oppose the marriage because she was afraid that if Cathy left Jim, she would just seek out still another abusive relationship. At least Jim was not being physically abusive. And he was Tammy's father. If Cathy married someone else, he might hurt Cathy or Tammy. Jim might be bad — the next relationship might be worse.

When Tammy was six, Cathy had another child — a boy they named James. Lorraine heard Jim say he never liked his name, none the less they named the boy after his father. She noticed that they hadn't named their daughter after the mother. Lorraine held her tongue. She got very good at that over the years.

Once again Jim demanded that Cathy go back to work before she had fully recouped from her second C Section. He told her they had four mouths to feed now. Without her income they wouldn't be able to put food on the table.

Obedient as ever, Cathy went back to work. Actually she looked forward to returning to work. Work had become an escape for her. She liked her boss, the other waitresses, her regular customers. She missed them all when she was on maternity leave. They were the family that was she missing in her life. Besides, going to work was better than staying at home and listening to Jim criticize her.

Recuperating from the surgery seemed harder than the first time. Cathy really wasn't up to working so soon after the delivery. She put in a few hours, then had to leave. When she got home she found the baby asleep in his bassinet in the living room. She didn't see Jim, but she heard him laughing from the bedroom. When she opened the door she found Jim in bed with the next door neighbor!

Cathy took the children and moved in with her mother. Within a few months, she filed for divorce. Jim demanded joint custody of the children. Cathy didn't argue the point. In her eyes, he may have been a terrible husband, still he was a good father. Just as she didn't seem to notice the verbal abuse he had heaped on her, Cathy didn't seem to notice how much time Jim spent criticizing Tammy. In Cathy's brainwashed eyes, Jim was a good father.

The judge gave them joint custody of the children with Cathy caring for them during the week and Jim having them on the weekends. Even though Jim had no job at the time, the judge ordered him to pay half of cost of the children's maintenance.

Without Cathy to support him, Jim had to get a job. He worked in locally for a while. He told Cathy the pay wasn't enough to support himself, forget about paying child support. He took off to Las Vegas trying to find a better paying job. He promised to send money for kids as soon as he was able.

He never did. Good, understanding, Cathy did not pursue the issue and raised the children on her waitress wages.

Lorraine didn't criticize Cathy for not making Jim contribute to the care of his children. She was just happy that Jim was out of their lives. And she was proud of Cathy. Somehow this second divorce made her grow up. Cathy said that the thing she had dreaded all these years (the break up of her marriage) wasn't so bad after all. She wasn't so tired anymore. She told her mother, "I spent more energy avoiding the problem than it took to do something about it."

Cathy began to take control of her life. She could indeed handle money. It wasn't that hard now that she didn't need to keep Jim in cigarettes and beer. Once separated, Cathy realized just how unhappy she had been. For the first time in a very long time she was happy.

Lorraine was happy as well. She cared for the children when Cathy worked. She was delighted to finally be allowed to be the grandmother she always wanted to be.

That happiness ended a few years later for both of them.

It was one a.m. when Cathy left work. She was almost home when a Hummer ran a stop sign and hit her square on the driver's side. Lorraine was a light sleeper and heard the noise. First the crash, then the emergency fire truck horns and police car sirens. She grabbed her robe and ran out. She collapsed when she saw it was Cathy.

Lorraine was inconsolable. The only reason she was able to pull herself together was to care for the children. Tammy at 14, and Jimmy at 8, needed her. She was all they had. And there was the matter of the lawsuit. The driver of the Hummer was the 17 year old child of a very wealthy family. Police arrested him at the scene for being under the influence. It was up to Lorraine to hire a Personal Injury attorney to sue for Cathy's wrongful death.

David was a young, cheerful, good-looking, up and coming lawyer. He explained the state's wrongful death statute to Lorraine, "Any family member can initiate a lawsuit for a wrongful death, however it's best to have you appointed as the Personal Representative of your daughter's Estate and sue on behalf of all of the members of your family who suffered from this loss."

Lorraine asked, "Cathy was divorced. Is her Ex entitled to any part of the lawsuit?"

"The Court will decide how much each member of the family is entitled to receive from the proceeds of the lawsuit. Jim is no longer a member of Cathy's family. He's not entitled to anything, unless Cathy was obliged to pay alimony to him."

"No. He was supposed to pay her child support — which he never did."

David went on to explain that they would be filing two lawsuits — one against the driver, and the other against the owner of the car, "Not only can you sue the driver of the Hummer for his negligence in running the stop sign and causing Cathy's death, you can sue his parents as well. It was their car. They gave him the keys to the car. They must have known he had a drinking problem. This lawsuit should be worth millions."

"Really?" Lorraine asked.

"Absolutely. After you called for an appointment, I read the police report showing that the driver and the other teenagers in the car were really stoned. The newspapers are all over this story because his parents are socialites."

Lorraine asked, "How do we get started?"

David said, "I'll start working on the drafts of the two lawsuits. You'll need to be appointed as Personal Representative. State law requires a Guardian to be appointed whenever a minor receives more than $10,000 as a result of lawsuit. You may want to begin to start the guardianship procedures at the same time you apply to be Personal Representative. I don't do probate or guardianship. I can recommend Amy Pohl, she's an Elder Law attorney."

And that's how I came to meet Lorraine.

While David had discounted Cathy's ex-husband as not being entitled to any part of the award, I knew Jim was sure to appear as the "concerned" and "loving" father of his two, soon to be very rich, children. No doubt other "loving" relatives would appear and file their own petition to be appointed Guardian.

I expressed these concerns to Lorraine.

Lorraine agreed, "You're right. Jim's sure to try to get control of the kid's money. That doesn't worry me so much as losing custody of the kid. He can't taking the kids away from me, can he?"

"That could be a problem," I answered, "Unless some Court terminated his rights as parent, James as the natural parent, has the right to take care of his children. What custody arrangements were made when they divorced?"

"They were awarded joint custody. But he never took them once. Jimmy was a baby when his father left. Tammy was six. She barely remembers him."

I said, "From what I'm hearing about James, he'll just be interested in the money. If we can get you appointed as Guardian of the property inherited by your grandchildren, he may not push all that hard to take on the responsibility of raising two children."

Lorraine worried, "He might want to take them from me just for spite. Can't we ask the judge to let me keep the children?"

"We could file to have you appointed as Guardian of the personal needs of the children at the same time that we file to have you appointed as the Guardian of their property. The problem with that strategy is that, in effect, we'd be asking to terminate Jim's rights as a parent. Terminating parental rights is hard to do. We would need to prove that he abandoned or severely abused the children."

"What about the fact that he never contributed to their support, or even visited them in all these years?"

"Yes, that's abandonment, however without Cathy here to testify that he never called, or sent her money, that might be hard to prove. She never asked the Court to enforce the child support. James will probably say that he sent cash to Cathy and regularly called her to see that the kids were OK."

I offered an alternative. "Maybe we should hold off asking for you to be the Guardian of the personal needs of your grandchildren. We could be worrying for nothing. James may not want to be a full-time dad. He may want to keep the kids with you."

Lorraine thought that might work, "He's never shown any interest in them. I'll tell him that he can visit them at any time. It'll be easier for him, if he just lets me keep on taking care of them."

"That's a good plan. It'll help if you can establish good relations with him. Once I file the petition for guardian-ship, the clerk will send him Notice of the hearing and a copy of your petition to be Guardian. You may want to call him to tell him to expect the Notice in the mail. You can explain what happened and why you are asking to be Guardian of their property."

The next day, I went to court and had Lorraine appointed as Personal Representative. Having her appointed Guardian would be harder. As I predicted, Jim filed a petition to be appointed as Guardian of his children's property. His mother filed her own petition to be appointed as the children's Guardian.

Judge Wecco appointed an attorney to represent Tammy as Guardian Ad Litem in the upcoming guardianship hearing. He appointed another attorney as Jimmy's Guardian Ad Litem. His order of appointment instructed each attorney to conduct an examination and file a report giving the children's history, their environment, their school record, their relationships, and to identify any special needs the children might have.

I received a call from my friend Susan. She was appointed as Tammy's Guardian Ad Litem. "I've been reading the petitions filed by your client and the father and the one filed by his mother. That guy sounds like a real loser."

"Yeah. He hasn't seen Tammy in eight years. He hasn't seen Jimmy since he was born. I'll bet he couldn't pick out his own son in a playground."

Susan asked whether the paternal grandmother was any more attentive to the children than her son.

"I don't know. You'll have to ask Lorraine. Jim's mother lives in another state, so I doubt if she spent any time visiting with them. Lorraine has been caring for the children these past eight years while Cathy was at work. It should be a no-brainer even for Wecco."

Susan cautioned, "Don't count on it. Wecco is pro-father. When he was in Family Court, he refused to terminate a father's parental rights even though the guy was a druggie who beat his wife. I heard that Wecco said 'I don't care if this guy is Charles Manson. It's his child and he has a right to be with that child!'."

"Sounds like classic Wecco."

"Yup," Susan agreed.

I felt confident that Tammy would want to have her grandmother as Guardian of her property, so I asked Susan to let Tammy be present at the hearing. "Tammy's 14 years old. State statute requires the judge to consider the preference of a child who is 14 or older."

Susan said, "In the few cases I've had before Wecco that involved a minor, he didn't seem interested in what the child had to say. Still it couldn't hurt to have her testify."

I received the reports filed by the Guardians Ad Litem and Court Investigator. The three reports said much the same thing. The children were well cared for by their maternal grandmother. They were doing well in school even though they were still grieving for their mother and had feelings of anger and sadness. The Court Investigator recommended that the children receive professional counseling to get them through this grieving period. Based on Jim's non existent record of child support, he recommended that Lorraine serve as Guardian of the children's property.

Once all the reports were filed, the guardianship hearing was scheduled.

The small courtroom was almost filled to capacity. There was Jim, his lawyer, his mother and her lawyer, the two Guardians Ad Litem, the Court Investigator, myself, Lorraine and the children. David was there on behalf of Lorraine in her role as Personal Representative. David filed a petition for permission to proceed with a lawsuit for Cathy's wrongful death on behalf of the children. David's petition was probably going to be uncontested, so the judge allowed it to be heard on the same day as the guardianship hearing.

Because the lawsuit involved prominent members of the county, the media was also present in the courtroom that day.

Even though everyone was well behind Wecco's famous red line, he still seemed uncomfortable with all these people crowding his court room. He said sternly "Anyone who makes any kind of noise will be escorted out by the bailiff!"

The courtroom was respectfully silent when the judge entered the courtroom, so his comment about noise was unprovoked. Those who had never been before this judge prior to this hearing, looked puzzled.

Each party got an opportunity to present his case. Jim's mother testified against her son. She said that Jim should not be Guardian because of his heavy drinking. He never finished high school. He never held a steady job. He worked nights as a drummer when work happened to be available. She was equally critical of Lorraine. She said Jim could have worked out his marital problems if his mother-in-law hadn't interfered. She said that Lorraine may have finished high school, however she had no experience in managing money. "I, on the other hand, have a college degree in liberal arts, so I am best qualified to be Guardian."

Jim appeared clean shaven, dark suit, shirt and tie. He was a tall, good looking man and made an impressive appearance on the witness stand. He testified that he regularly called Cathy and that they were on very good terms right up to the time she died. He admitted that he was a bit behind in his child support payments. He said he fully intended to make support payments current now that he had steady work at a night club.

Wecco was particularly courteous to Jim, asking him how he would manage the children's property if he continued to live in Las Vegas. That courtesy was not a good sign for our side.

Judge Wecco said to Jim "As a parent, you can serve as Guardian of the property of a child even though you live in another state. You'll need to send the money to the children's grandmother to support the children, and you will need to account to the Court every year for money you spend on their behalf."

Jim noticeably relaxed in the witness chair. It was obvious that the judge was on his side. To assure the judge that he would be a good Guardian and parent, Jim said "That won't be a problem. In fact, as soon as the case is settled, I'll probably have the children come and live with me in Las Vegas."

Tammy grabbed her grandmother and screamed "No. No. You can't let him take me away from Nana. He used to beat me when I was a little girl. He hurt me. He hurt me bad. He'll hurt my little brother, too!"

Jimmy saw his sister's distress and started crying loudly.

James jumped to his feet, shouting that he never, ever, struck Tammy. His mother came to his defense and yelled out, "My son would never strike his child. He's not like that."

Judge Wecco pounded his gavel and demanded order in the court. He told the Guardians Ad Litem to remove the children to the waiting room.

Once the courtroom settled down, I rose to my feet and asked for permission to make a speaking petition. "Your Honor, there are petitions before this Court for the appointment of a Guardian of the property for each child, however none for a Guardian of their person. My client wishes to file a petition to be appointed as the Temporary Guardian for their person. The children have been living with their grandmother since the divorce eight years ago. According to his own testimony, their father has not seen his children in all this time, nor has he contributed to their support. This constitutes abandonment of his children."

The judge didn't seem convinced, so I continued, "The law allows the Court to appoint a Temporary Guardian when it appears there may be a danger to the health and well being of the child. His own mother testified that he's been drinking since he was a teenager. Obviously, when he drinks, he is physically abusive. Tammy's testimony is convincing evidence such abuse."

Knowing Wecco's reputation for being reluctant to terminate a father's rights, I offered a way for the father to regain custody of his children. "Appointing a Temporary Guardian does not terminate parental rights. This Court may allow supervised visitation rights. The father may petition the Court to modify or terminate this order whenever he can present evidence to the Court that he can be a fit parent."

The judge nodded his heard in approval. He directed me to put my petition in writing. He said to the attorney who represented Jim and the attorney representing Jim's mother, "You will have ten days to respond to Mrs. Pohl's written petition."

He said to Lorraine, "I am granting your petition to serve as the Guardian of the property of your grandchildren."

He said to David, "I'm granting your petition to file a lawsuit on behalf of the children.

He banged his gavel and said, "This Court is adjourned." He got up and walked out of the courtroom.

Once I left the courtroom I was able to comfort the children, telling them that their grandmother was now the Guardian of their property and that the judge was seriously considering letting them stay with their grandmother.

I called Lorraine the next day, "Did you know that Jim was beating Tammy?"

"No. Cathy never said he hit her. I never saw anything that would make me believe he was violent. Nasty, yes. Violent, I don't think so. I thought you told her to say that so we would win."

I was more than annoyed. How could Lorraine think me capable of doing such a thing? I thought she knew me better than that. "No. I would never coach Tammy to lie in court. That would be telling her to commit perjury. That's a crime. That would be a terrible thing to do to a child."

Lorraine said, "Then I guess it must be true. I never suspected."

The following month I called with the good news that the judge had granted my petition. He appointed Lorraine as Temporary Guardian of the children's personal needs until further order of the Court or their 18th birthday, whichever was the earlier date.

I told Lorraine, "This order is a good thing to have in case there is some emergency such as giving permission for treatment in the event one of the children takes sick. Without this order, you would have had to contact Jim to get his permission for medical treatment."

"That doesn't seem right. What if I couldn't reach him?"

"Most doctors allow a grandparent to consent to emergency medical treatment if the child's parent, or stepparent is not available. This order saves the time of trying to locate the parent."

As it turned out, the petition may not have been necessary to keep the children with Lorraine. Once she was appointed as Guardian of the children's property, Jim and his mother lost interest in the case. They didn't bother to have their lawyers respond to my petition. I doubted whether the children would ever hear from their father again.

And they never did.

Chapter 7a   Guardian Angel

"No need to beware the good child with Tammy," thought Lorraine. Every day it was something new, starting with the day Tammy found out that Judge Wecco granted Lorraine's Petition For Appointment of Temporary Guardian.

"Played that judge like a guitar," bragged Tammy.

"What are you talking about?" asked Lorraine.

"I saw that my father was going to win, so I gave the judge my best performance. I learned how it's done on T.V."

Lorraine was having trouble grasping what Tammy was saying, "You mean you lied about your father beating you?"

"I don't really remember him all that much. I remember he yelled at me a lot. I don't remember him beating me." She shrugged her shoulder, "Maybe he did."

"Why did you say that he did that?"

"He was going to take me to Las Vegas. I don't want to go there. I live here. All my friends are here. My school is here. If I had to live with him, I'd just have to run away."

Lorraine told me about Tammy's admission when she came to my office to sign the forms that we needed to submit to the Court as the children's Guardian.

Lorraine was in tears, "She didn't pull that courtroom act because she wanted to live with me. She doesn't care about me. Her friends are her whole life. She lives on the telephone. That's when she's home. All she wants to do is hang out with her friends. I have to fight to get her home by 8 o'clock to do her homework for the next day. Her grades are going down. She just doesn't care."

I saw things differently, "Tammy is one bright, spunky kid. Imagine her figuring out how the judge was going to rule, then figuring out the consequences of that ruling, and then going into an act to get her way! I believe she very much cares for you. I saw her interaction with you in the courtroom. She was glued to your side. Body language tells me more than the spoken word. Look at things from Tammy's perspective. Her parents were divorced when she was six and her father disappeared from her life. No letters. No phone calls. Nothing. Then her mother is killed when she is 14. Her father reappears as soon as he finds that she's going to be worth a lot of money. No wonder she wants no part of him. The report of the Court Investigator said that both she and Jimmy are angry and grieving for their mother. He recommended you all attend grief counseling."

"Yeah. But he didn't say how I am supposed to pay for it. I don't know how long this case is going to drag on."

I offered to call David and see if I could speed things up.

I told David that Lorraine was having a difficult time trying to support the two children, "Do you think you can get the defendants to begin to talk settlement?"

David thought that was a bad idea.

He explained, "I haven't completed my discovery of the events that took place. The parents are the ones with the money. I need to establish that it was more their fault than their son's. The few facts I collected so far point in that direction. They gave him a sports car when he was 16. He wrapped it around a telephone pole before he was 17. Since then he's been driving his mother's Mercedes. His dad bought this Hummer a few weeks ago before the accident. Junior decided to show it off and drive his friends to a party. I suspect that they gave their son no special training in how to handle an oversized car. The accident happened on the way back from the party. If I can prove that the parents knew, or should have known, that their son would be drinking at the party, we can double the award."

"Looks like it may take years to settle this case," I said.

David said, "Probably. The parents employed a big law firm to defend themselves. Their lawyer would love me to start talking settlement before I can get damaging evidence against his clients. No. Trying to quickly settle this case would be the worse thing we could do."

I agreed with David and told him I would explain the problem it to Lorraine.

I told Lorraine what David said during her next office visit. She said, "I understand, but that doesn't help pay the bills."

I asked, "Has Jim been sending support payments for the children?"

"Silly question," she chided.

"Of course," I agreed. "What was I thinking?"

I suggested forcing him to pay, "I could file a petition in Family Court requiring Jim to make his support payments current."

Lorraine looked worried, "No. If we start demanding money, he'll could try to get the children. I'm just a Temporary Guardian of their person. Jim could go back to court and demand that they live with him."

"You're right. But you still need money for the children's support. What about taking out an equity loan on your home? I can ask the Court to allow you to borrow money on behalf of the children, this way you will be able to pay off the loan as soon as the case is settled."

"No," Lorraine said. "That just gives me the problem of trying to pay a mortgage each month. I heard about a reverse mortgage on T.V. The ad said they will pay me each month. I called and they sent me a brochure. From what I can see the house will be worth less when I die. The kids are going to inherit this house anyway. I'd rather they use the money now when they need, it instead of after I die."

"OK. Just keep a record of all of the money you are spending to support the children. I'll see that you are reimbursed from the settlement. You are also entitled to be paid for taking care of the children, and for all of the time and money you spent to be appointed Guardian."

Lorraine said she was not interested in being paid. "These are my grandchildren. I took care of them when Cathy went to work. I didn't charge then. I won't charge now. That's the most I can do for my Cathy."

I could see that Lorraine was on the brink of tears, so I didn't pursue the matter any further.

Lorraine did get the reverse mortgage, still even that was not enough to support two growing children. She got a job working in the school cafeteria. The job worked out well. She worked when the children were in school and she was home when they were home.

It took almost three years before we got down to serious settlement talks. The judge in charge of the wrongful death action ordered the parties to attend mediation before he would schedule a trial. The lawyers took weeks squabbling over who should serve as mediator, fearing that anyone chosen by the other side might be partial to that side. Finally, they found a mediator who never worked with any of the law firms. In addition to his work as mediator, he was an experienced trial attorney, so he had a good idea of the strengths and weaknesses of each side.

The conference was held in the mediator's office. The children's Guardians Ad Litem were there. I appeared as attorney for Lorraine in her role as the children's Guardian. Two attorneys were there from the law firm representing the parents of the driver. Another attorney, from a different law firm, was there representing their son. All of the defendants were present.

The first two hours were spent with each side presenting their case to the mediator. We then separated into different rooms with the mediator going back and forth all morning trying to get each side to agree to settle. The mediator had lunch brought in so that the parties could continue to work towards a settlement.

Late in the afternoon, the parties agreed upon a settlement value and were ready to talk about the structure of the settlement. That's when the Guardians Ad Litem and I began to participate. We agreed that a lump sum settlement would not be in the children's best interest. Handing them a chunk of money when they turned 18 would be a bad idea. Instead we worked out a payment schedule for each child so that (s)he would receive enough to get through college, and then receive annual payments thereafter over a period of ten years. Any sum left over from that child's half of the settlement would be given to the child when (s)he reached the age of 40. The money would be managed and distributed by a trust company chosen by Lorraine, as the children's Guardian.

The total settlement was approximately 3.5 million dollars. After David received his one-third contingency fee and all of the costs of the case were paid, each child received an award of just over a million dollars.

Once the lawsuit was over, the guardianships settled into a routine. Lorraine kept in touch with me on a regular basis. Raising two teenagers was difficult for this aging grandmother. Knowing that I was a mother myself, she sought my counsel when parenting got rough. "I found what I thought was a cigarette in Jimmy's room. Tammy told me it's not a cigarette. It's a joint. You know, marijuana. I grounded him for a month and he's not allowed to hang out with that friend who got him to try pot. Still I'm worried sick. I never had these problems when Cathy was growing up. She was such a good child."

I wondered, "Didn't you take the kids to grief counseling a while back?"

"Yes, we all went together and then separately."

I asked, "Did it help?"

"I guess" Lorraine said, "but Jimmy hated it. He said he didn't like to talk about his feelings and that's all the psychologist wanted to do."

"You might tell him that if he ever does this again, you will all need to go back to counseling."

Lorraine laughed, "That ought to straighten him right up. Who said counseling doesn't work?"

FIVE YEARS LATER

Lorraine called and asked, "Do you know who's birthday is coming up in two weeks?"

"Actually, I do. It's on my calendar that Jimmy's guardianship is terminating because he's turning 18. I'll need to prepare your final report and Petition For Discharge as the Guardian of Jimmy's property. We'll also ask for the Court to discharge you as the Temporary Guardian of his person.

Lorraine suggested, "Let's celebrate Jimmy's birthday by going to court, getting me discharged as Guardian, and then to a nice restaurant."

"Great. I'll put the forms in the mail for you to sign. They're easy to complete. They're the same as you signed when Tammy turned 18. Once I receive them back from you, I'll file it with the court and have the clerk schedule a hearing with the judge."

I met Lorraine at the court house. She was with Tammy and Jimmy. Everyone looked so different than when I first met them. Tammy, at 24, was a grown woman. She was in her second year of law school. One more year, and she would be an attorney. Spunky as ever. I knew she would make an excellent lawyer. Jimmy had grown into quite the man. I wondered (however didn't ask) whether Lorraine noticed how much he looked like his father.

Lorraine looked pale, almost fragile. I knew she had been battling cancer on and off for years. Each time she thought she had it cured, it reoccurred in a different place. Each round of treatment seemed harder than the last. As I looked at her, a sadness came over me. I feared this battle would be her last.

But this day we were all smiles. It was indeed a day to celebrate.

When we entered the courtroom, Lorraine asked, "Is this the same courtroom? It looks different."

I laughed. "It's the same, however Judge Wecco is gone. He was transferred to criminal court."

Lorraine said, "Poor criminals."

"No" I said, "Poor prosecutors. That judge was never able to tell the good guys from the bad guys. The prosecutors will have a hard time convincing Wecco that anyone should go to jail. I wonder if he's going to keep the prosecutors behind a red line."

"What red line?" Lorraine asked.

"Don't you remember the red line he had on the floor? No one was allowed to step over that line without his permission. As you will see in a few minutes, this judge is nothing like Wecco."

Judge Bennett came in. No fanfare. Just a nice smile to everyone and a greeting, "Good morning, I see by this petition that you're here today because this young man is now 18 years old and no longer in need of a Temporary Guardian of his person, or as Guardian of his property."

We all smiled back and nodded in agreement.

The judge said, "I've been looking through this file. It goes back some ten years, yet I have not been able to find any money spent for the care of the Ward, nor do I find any money paid to the Guardian for the care she has given over the years. In fact, the structured settlement appears to be significantly greater in value than it was when it was approved by the Court over eight years ago."

We all smiled and once again nodded in agreement.

The judge wasn't sure if I understood that he was asking a question, "Mrs. Pohl, are you telling me that the Guardian used her own money to support her Ward and hasn't taken any compensation for the care she gave to her Ward for the past ten years?"

I nodded 'yes', and was about to answer when Lorraine spoke up, "He's my grandson. Why would I want to charge him for doing something that has given me so much happiness these past years? Besides even if I did get paid, everything I own will go to him and his sister, anyway. They're my only family. I just didn't see the point of taking any money."

Judge Bennett shook his head and said, "Never in all my years on the bench have I seen such selfless dedication." He looked at Jimmy, "Young man, you are very fortunate to have this woman as your grandmother. I hope you appreciate her."

With shoulders back, Jimmy said, "Yes, sir. I surely do."

Judge Bennett smiled, signed the order, and wished us good luck as we left the courtroom.

Lorraine was surprised, "That's a different kind of judge."

"No." I said, "It was Wecco who was the different kind of judge."

THREE MONTHS LATER

As I suspected, Lorraine's health was on a downward spiral. Tammy told me that her grandmother refused to enter Hospice until Jimmy was settled in his dorm at the University.

Just before Lorraine died, she asked Tammy to promise to take good care of her brother. Tammy said she didn't know if Nana heard the promise because she closed her eyes and was gone.

I told Tammy that I was sure she did.

I don't usually attend the funeral of someone who had been my client, however Lorraine was different. She and I became close friends over the ten years she served as Guardian.

There were few people at Lorraine's funeral service. There were only two cars following the hearse to the cemetery. I thought there should be more cars, more people. People should know that a wonderful person died. But Tammy knew, and Jimmy knew, and I knew, and maybe that's all that really counted.

At the grave site, we were well composed, yet each of us was fighting back tears.

Tammy tried to console herself. "Now she's in heaven with Mom."

Jimmy had a cheering thought, "Now she's our Guardian Angel!"

We all smiled.

I said, "That's what she's always been."

Part II

Avoiding Guardianship

After reading these past seven chapters, you now have a good understanding of how guardianship works. You probably have concluded that guardianship has few, if any, redeeming features and are thinking:

Everyone should take steps to avoid guardianship.

The next logical question is how do you do it?

Maybe the best way to answer that question is to go back to each story and figure out how guardianship could have been avoided in the first place.

It's a story rewind — only rewritten and then played back with the main character understanding the importance of avoiding guardianship and then taking steps to do so.

Chapter 1 Rewrite

Avoiding Guardianship For The Elderly

The story described in Chapter 1 of this book is probably the most common guardianship scenario. A single person who is elderly (Virginia) comes down with a debilitating disease (Alzheimer's). A close family member (Walter) has been helping her with her finances. When she is no longer able to sign her name, he needs to get legal authority (guardianship) to conduct business on her behalf.

I don't know what upset Walter more, the cost of the guardianship, or the fact that once established, the judge and not Walter was in charge of his sister's fate. The judge made it very clear that if Walter didn't follow court rules (having his lawyer sign the reports) the judge would remove Walter as Guardian and give the job to a perfect stranger. Walter had to submit. He had no choice.

The first lesson to be learned from this chapter is:
Once a person is found to be legally incapacitated,
it's the judge and not the family,
who is in control of the Ward.

Although following court rules made Walter bridle, the thing he most complained about was the cost of guardianship. And why wouldn't he? Every penny he spent on guardianship was just that much less for him to inherit.

When Virginia died, probate was a simple matter. Because there was a valid Will and only one beneficiary, I was able transfer the house to Walter within a few months for a fraction of what it cost for the guardianship.

Which leads to the second point of the story.

It is more important to avoid guardianship than it is to avoid probate.

MAYBE IT WAS MY FAULT

Before Virginia took ill, she and Walter came to me to draft their respective Wills. At that time, I discussed the importance of a Power of Attorney, however they said they only wanted Wills. It isn't my style to be pushy, so I let it go. Looking back now, I realize that it may have been just as much my fault as my clients' for not taking steps to avoid guardianship. I should have insisted. I should have spent more time trying to convince them of the importance of a Power of Attorney.

Perhaps more as a catharsis to me, let's go back and rewrite history. This time we're all going to get it right!

THE POWER OF ATTORNEY

Walter and Virginia made an appointment to come in and write out their Wills. I immediately knew they were siblings. Both were about the same height. Both were fair, grey haired, with grey-blue eyes. They had square, jowly faces. The wrinkles about their eyes told me they probably had a good sense of humor. I asked if they were twins.

They laughed and Virginia said, "No. He's my kid brother."

I would have guessed that he was older, because he seemed to be the dominant one. He directed Virginia into the room and pulled out a chair for her to sit on. He said, "We want Wills. My wife is gone, and so is her husband. We never had children. We only have each other here. We have two cousins in New York. If I die, I want everything to go to my sister. If she dies before me, I want to give what I have to my cousins, equally."

Virginia nodded her head, "Yes, I want the same thing."

When we finished drafting the Wills, I said, "To complete your Estate Plan, it is important for each of you to sign a Power of Attorney."

Virginia protested, "I don't have an Estate. I just have a house and a few stocks."

I explained, "Your Estate is everything you own. An Estate Plan provides for the care of your property during your life time making sure that your property is managed properly in the event you are too sick to handle your finance. The Plan also provides for the distribution of your property once you die."

Virginia said, "I have a joint account with Walter. If I get sick he can pay my bills from my account."

"If you're sick a long time that money might run out and he might need to cash in your securities."

"So I'll make the securities joint."

I said, "If you do that, you'll be making a gift of half of the stocks to Walter. If half of the value of your securities are over $12,000, you'll need to file a federal gift tax return."

Virginia asked, "You mean I have to pay taxes?"

"No. Not unless you're transferring over your life-time gift tax limit, which is currently one million dollars."

Virginia laughed, "I'm no millionaire."

I said, "There's still the problem of the house. You might come down with a lengthy illness, such as Alzheimer's or Parkinson's and need to live in a nursing home. That could happen. Statistics show that the probability of having dementia increases as we age. By age 85, we have a 50% chance of suffering some degree of dementia.

"I could put the house in Walter's name too."

I didn't think that was a good idea. "Residents of this state have tax breaks for those people who occupy their home as their primary residence. If you make a gift of half of your home, it may cost you more in taxes to live in your own home. And putting the house in both of your names won't solve the problem of being able to transfer the house if it needed to be sold. As joint owner, Walter could only agree to selling his half. He couldn't sell your half. "

I suggested, "You're making the problem too hard. There's a simple solution. Give Walter a Durable Power of Attorney."

I could see that Virginia was not familiar with a Power of Attorney so I went on to explain, "A Durable Power of Attorney is a document that you (the *Principal*) sign giving someone (your *Agent* or *Attorney-In-Fact*) authority to handle your finances. The word *durable* means that Walter can continue to use the Power of Attorney, regardless of whether you later become incapacitated. If you give Walter a *General* Power of Attorney, he can do much the same with your finances as you can."

"You mean I won't be able to take care of my own money?"

I assured her, "You're free to take care of your finances just as you always do. If the time comes that you are too sick to take care of your finances, Walter can use the Durable Power of Attorney to do whatever business that needs to be done for you. Pay your bills. Make repairs to your condo if needed. He won't be able to use the Power of Attorney unless he has possession of the original document. You can keep the Power of Attorney in your house. All you need to do is to tell Walter where it is so that he can find it in the event of an emergency."

"That makes sense," said Virginia. "You can make me a Power of Attorney."

Walter chimed in, "You can make one for me too."

THE HEALTH CARE DIRECTIVE

I went on to discuss making provision for her health care, "The Power of Attorney takes care of your finances in the event you're ill, however it doesn't take care of your medical decisions in case you're not able to tell the doctors what treatment you do, or do not, want."

Virginia said, "You mean a Living Will? I already have one of those. I went to the hospital for some surgery and they gave me a form that I signed."

I explained, "A Living Will says whether you do (or do not) want life support systems to be used in the event that you are dying and there is no hope for your recovery, or if you're in a coma with no hope of ever waking up. Giving written instructions about the care you wish to receive is important. Equally important is to give someone authority to carry out your wishes."

Virginia said, "If I get that sick, my brother will tell the doctors what to do."

I agreed with her, "In most states, including this one, there is an order of priority for making health care decisions for a loved one who is unable to direct his health care. For an adult, that person is his spouse."

She reminded me that she wasn't married.

"Yes, I know. I'm just telling you who doctors would ask permission for treatment. In the absence of a spouse, they would ask the children."

"I don't have children, but it seems to me that wouldn't be a good idea. What if the children disagreed about the treatment, who would the doctor listen to?"

"In that case, they would have to go to court and ask the judge to appoint one of them as Guardian. That's why it is important that the parent appoint one of his children as Health Care Agent."

Walter was getting annoyed with all of these hypotheticals. "All that is well and good, but she has only one brother that's me."

I agreed, "You would tell the doctors that you have top priority, because she has no spouse or child or any other family member to speak for her. But suppose you both were injured in a car accident, who would be there to speak for you?"

Virginia answered, "That would be my cousin in New York."

I asked, "Which cousin? You have two, And how is the doctor supposed to know how to contact him? If you are in an emergency situation, how is anyone supposed to know about your cousin in New York. It is important to appoint Walter as your Health Care Agent and an alternate in the event Walter is unable to speak for you. You can do this by signing a *Health Care Directive*."

Virginia said, "All right, all right. Make the Health Care Directive. I think this is going to be one big bill."

"If cost is of concern, you can use the Internet to prepare your own documents. All you need to do is use your favorite search engine and type in Health Care Directive. You should also type in the name of this state. Many states have statutory Health Care Directives that you can download without cost. You can do the same to prepare your own Durable Power of Attorney."

Virginia thought about it and decided to have me prepare the Health Care Directive and the Durable Power of Attorney. "I'm not too good on the computer. It's easier if you do it for me."

Walter wondered "Why do you need to prepare two documents? Can't you just give me the right to make her medical decisions as part of her Power of Attorney?"

"I could, however, as a practical matter, it's better to have a separate Health Care Directive. Two documents give you have more flexibility. You may want one person to serve as your Health Care Agent and another to serve as your Attorney-In-Fact for business matters. One family member may be an excellent choice to make your health care decisions, yet that person may not be the best person to make your financial decisions."

"No." Virginia said, "I want Walter to make all my decisions."

I still thought separate documents were better, "Even if you want Walter as your Health Care Agent and your Attorney-In-Fact, there is still the matter of privacy. You will give a copy of your Health Care Directive to your physician to be placed in your medical file. Your doctors have no need to know of your business arrangements and vice versa. To conduct business on your behalf, your brother will need to give a copy of the Durable Power of Attorney to people you do business with (banks, stockbrokers, etc.). They have no need to know of your medical decisions. For privacy, and perhaps security reasons, it's better to have two separate documents, rather than try to get it all into a single multi-purpose document."

Walter and Virginia agreed to have me prepare Estate planning documents for each of them. I prepare drafts of the documents within the week, and mailed them off for each to review before signing.

During their next office visit, they signed the documents and went off with their respective Wills, Durable Powers of Attorney and Health Care Directives.

I was happy knowing that I did a good job – this time.

YEARS LATER

Walter came in for an appointment some years later. He looked older than when I saw him last. Thinner, more bent over. His forehead wrinkled into permanent worry lines.

"Good to see you, Walter. How have you been? How's Virginia?"

"Not too well. She came down with Alzheimer's. I've been taking care of her at home. Now that she needs 24 hour care, I was thinking of having her stay at Happy Oaks."

"That's a nice place. Virginia will be well cared for there."

"Yeah, but it's expensive. I'll need to cash in her securities. Here is the Power of Attorney she signed. You said I could use it to sell her securities."

I explained how to use it, "Go to your stockbroker and show him your Power of Attorney. You can give him a copy. Don't give him the original document. There's only one original and you need to keep it in your possession. He may want you to sign an Affidavit saying that the Power of Attorney is still in effect and that Virginia did not revoke that Power of Attorney."

Walter said, "Do brokers have Affidavit forms in their office?"

"Generally they do. I'll prepare a few Affidavits for you in case you need to use the Durable Power of Attorney to sell the stocks or for any other reason."

"OK. Thank you."

"Virginia signed a Health Care Directive making you her Health Care Agent. You will want to make sure her doctor has a copy so that he knows that you will be making all of her health care decisions."

"I already did that."

Now being a conscientious attorney, I thought about the documents Walter signed. "As I remember, you also have a Health Care Directive. I know you named Virginia as your Health Care Agent. I don't recall who you named as alternate."

"My cousin in New York."

"You'll want to check that he has a copy of your Health Care Directive and is still willing to make your medical decisions in the event you can't."

I offered to draft a new Durable Power of Attorney for him. "Virginia won't be able to help with your finances should you take ill. Did you want to sign a new Power of Attorney appointing your cousin as your Attorney-In-Fact?"

Walter looked at me as if I'd lost my mind. "Look at all of the things this Power of Attorney gives me the right to do for Virginia:
— buy or sell her real property
— buy or sell her personal property
— trade in her securities (stocks, bonds, etc.)
— pay her bills and taxes
— operate any business she may own
— have access to her safe deposit box
— borrow money on her behalf
— buy insurance policies (with her money!)
    and name the beneficiary of my choice
— sue or defend a lawsuit on her behalf
— apply for government benefits on her behalf
— take money out of her retirement account.

I would let Virginia do these things for me. Not anyone else."

"Suppose you got sick like Virginia? If you don't give someone a Durable Power of Attorney to handle your finances, it will be necessary to have a Court appoint a Guardian to take care of your property."

"I'll worry about it when I get sick."

"That may be too late. You might not be able to sign your name. I can draft a Power of Attorney for you that cannot be used until and unless two doctors say that you are too ill to manage your finances. All I need to do is include a paragraph in the Power of Attorney that says:
    This Durable Power of Attorney becomes operational only when my regularly attending physician and another independent physician sign an Affidavit stating that I am disabled or incapacitated.

This is called a *Springing Power of Attorney*. Your Attorney-In-Fact can hold the original document, however he can't use it until it 'springs to life' when two doctors sign an Affidavit saying that you are disabled and too ill to care for your finances."

Walter said he would think about it. And he left.

When I thought about it, I could understand Walter's reluctance. By giving his cousin a Durable Power of Attorney, Walter would be making his cousin responsible to care for his finances in the event of his incapacity. No Court would oversee that care. His brother could handle Walter's finances without supervision from anyone. However, if Walter became incapacitated and didn't have a Power of Attorney, a judge would see to Walter's care. The judge would appoint a Guardian to care for Walter and his property. The Guardian would be supervised by the Court.

If it cost money to establish and maintain a guardianship for Walter's protection, there would be just that much less for his cousin to inherit. And that was fine with Walter.

Chapter 2 Rewrite

Avoiding Guardianship
For The Mentally Ill

A person who had been mentally ill for all of her adult life (Mollie) sold her home to someone who claimed to be her friend. Once Mollie sold the house, she took to living on the streets. Without her medication, she became a danger to herself and others. The police arrested her for assault and contacted her son, Paul.

The true facts of the sale are never discovered. At best it was a poor bargain for Mollie. At worst a scam. Paul became a Guardian of the property so that he could sue to recover the house. He became the Guardian of her person so that he could be in charge of her health care and living arrangements. The lawsuit was successful. Paul retrieved the house, however he had to sell it to pay for the cost of the lawsuit, the cost of the guardianship, and for Mollie's care while the lawsuit was in progress.

As the Guardian of the person, Paul had the right to decide where Mollie would live. That legal authority had little practical value. Mollie lived where she wanted to live. The law does not allow a Guardian to force a Ward to live anywhere. As Guardian of the person Paul had the authority to decide his mother's medical treatment. That legal authority was not effective unless Mollie cooperated and took her medicine — something she was not always willing to do. The law does not allow a Guardian to force-feed medication.

The point of this story is:
Guardianship of the person may not be effective for someone with severe mental illness.

Those who are determined to see the glass as half full may say, "At least they got Mollie's house back." Yet who profited? All of the lawyers for sure. That included the two lawyers who litigated the case, and the two guardianship lawyers, namely me and Mollie's lawyer, Richard. The court system also took its bite of the settlement pie.

Paul was paid for his expenses flying back and forth from D.C. to attend to the lawsuit and guardianship matters. He took a sizable fee for the many hours he spent in his role as Guardian.

Prior to the guardianship, Mollie's former husband was sending money to Paul to pay for Mollie's care. Once Paul became the Guardian of Mollie's property, he became responsible for her maintenance, so the former husband stopped sending money. Indirectly, Mollie's former husband profited from the sale of the house.

Mollie was the only one who did not profit financially by establishing a guardianship of her property.

The problem of the house all stemmed from the fact that Mollie's husband gave her the house as part of their divorce settlement. To rewrite this story to avoid guardianship, we need to go back to Mollie's divorce. Her husband knew she was too ill to handle alimony payments, so he gave money to Paul to take care of his mother. Her husband should have been astute enough to know that she was too ill to own real property as well.

There are any number of ways Mollie's husband could have allowed her to continue to live in the house without giving her the right to sell it. A relatively simple solution would have been to give her a Life Estate in the house, with the Remainder Interest to Paul. The divorce decree could have made the husband responsible to pay all costs associated with the home. By giving her a Life Estate, Mollie could go and come as she pleased, yet with a home that was always hers to come back to.

Let's pick up the story. Only this time, Mollie has a Life Estate in the property.

Paul came to my office because he was concerned about his mother. "She's at Mercy Hospital for evaluation and treatment. She's been living on the streets and not taking her medication."

I asked, "Where was she living before she was on the street?"

"She owns a Life Estate in a nice home. She tried to sell the house to someone who says he's her friend. When she found out that the deed was written so that she couldn't sell it without getting my permission, she let her friend live in the house and she took to the streets. When I discovered what she did, I evicted him. He left the place in a mess. I had it cleaned, so it's ready for her to move back as soon as she leaves the hospital."

"You seem to have things under control."

Paul disagreed, "No I don't. I don't have any authority to tell her where to live or to take her medicine or to not try to sell things she doesn't even own. I was thinking of becoming her Guardian."

I explained that guardianship wouldn't make taking care of his mother any easier. As an alternative, I recommended a Durable Power of Attorney. "The Power of Attorney will give you the right to conduct business on her behalf."

Paul didn't think that necessary, "She has no need to do business."

"Doing business includes applying for government benefits for your mother. It could happen that she is the victim of an accident or medical malpractice or some other wrongdoing. A Durable Power of Attorney will give you the right to sue on her behalf."

Paul wondered how Mollie could sign a Durable Power of Attorney when she was so "out of it."

I suggested, "A chronic illness, including mental illness, is not a static thing. There are good days and bad days. I can draft a Power of Attorney for your mother. You can bring her to my office to sign it any time she is willing and able to do so."

Paul agreed that having his mother sign a Durable Power of Attorney would be a good idea, however there was still the problem of keeping her off the streets and taking her medicine.

I explained that no legal document, and no ruling from a judge could force Mollie to do anything unless she was a danger to herself or others. "Your mother might agree to letting you serve as her Health Care Agent. That will give you the authority to make her health care decisions should it happen that she is too sick to do so herself. She can do this by signing a document called a Health Care Directive."

Paul thought that a good idea, "OK. Draft the Directive. She can sign it at the same time she comes in to sign the Power of Attorney."

I said that I couldn't draft a Health Care Directive without knowing what treatment Mollie wanted. "I need to know whether she wants to have life support systems turned off in the event she is terminally ill with no hope of recovery. If she does, I can include a Living Will as part of her Health Care Directive."

Paul said, "I'll ask her what she wants and I'll call you so that you can have the Directive ready to sign."

I was not comfortable with that arrangement. "No. I need to speak to your mother to make sure she understands what she is going to sign. I can represent you and your mother only if there is no conflict of interest. I know you want this Durable Power of Attorney and Health Care Directive for your mother's own good, however if I am going to represent Mollie, she needs to want these documents for herself. And she needs to want me to be her lawyer. You can bring her to my office. Once she agrees to having me as her lawyer, you'll need to go out to the waiting room until we complete the visit."

Paul said, "I'll try to explain all this to her. I don't know if she'll want any part of it."

I suggested, "Try to get her to understand that by signing the Durable Power of Attorney she will avoid the need to have someone appointed to serve as the Guardian of her property. By signing the Health Care Directive, she will avoid the need to have someone appointed to be the Guardian for her personal needs."

THE MENTAL HEALTH CARE DIRECTIVE

I guess Paul was successful in convincing his mother that she needed a Durable Power of Attorney and Health Care Directive, because she came into my office saying, "I'm ready to sign my Power of Attorney."

"That's fine. First Paul needs to go to the waiting room. I don't want anyone to say he, or anyone else, made you sign anything. I want you to sign a Power of Attorney because that's what <u>you</u> want to do."

Mollie gave me a surprised look. She expected me to be like everyone else and tell her what to do. She didn't expect me to be interested in what <u>she</u> had to say.

Once Paul left, she sat down and chatted with me. We soon became good buddies. I explained every line of the Durable Power of Attorney, and why it was important to have Paul available to assist her should the need arise. She said she wanted to sign. I called in my assistants to witness and notarize her signature.

We then turned to the Health Care Directive. I told her that I needed her input before I could complete the form "Do you want life support systems to be turned off if you are terminally ill with no hope of recovery?

"Oh honey, I wish I could turn off life support right now." Mollie then went on to explain about the evils of yellow.

I was concerned that she might not be well enough to sign any more documents this day, so I asked "Is yellow here now?"

"No, of course not. I'm on my meds."

She was well enough to understand that yellow was a product of her illness, so I continued. I asked her who she wished to make her medical decisions in the event she was too ill to make them herself. She chose Paul as her Health Care Agent, and her former husband as alternate.

Her next question to me was profound, "Can I put in this document what kind of treatment I want when I'm not myself?"

"Yes, you can. What directions do you want to give to your Health Care Agent?"

"It's more what I don't want. I don't want shock treatments. I was in a place once where someone was given that treatment. He came out of it looking like a zombie. I'm afraid some day some doctor will want to do that to me. That's why I don't trust doctors."

"I'll put in directions that under no circumstance are you ever to be given shock treatments of any kind, not electric shock, not chemical shock or any other type of treatment that might have the effect of destroying brain tissue. I'll even draft a document for Paul to sign saying that he understands that by accepting his role as Health Care Agent he is legally bound to see to it that your directions are followed."

I completed the Directive and Mollie signed it. I called Paul in to explain the document. He was surprised at the mental health instruction. He told his mother, "I didn't know you felt this way about shock treatments. Of course I'll sign the acceptance. I'll make sure that never happens to you."

Once the documents were signed, we said our good-byes and Mollie went off arm in arm with her son.

Chapter 3 Rewrite

Avoiding Guardianship For The Wealthy

A successful businessman (Ben) is driving home from work when his car rolls over an embankment. Severe head injuries leave him in a coma. His doctors want to transfer him to a nursing home, however his wife (Edeeshia) cannot access his bank account. It is necessary to have a Guardian of his property to manage his finances and a Guardian of his person to oversee his medical treatment.

There is a court battle over who should serve as Guardian. The Court Investigator recommends Ben's brother (John). The judge disregards the recommendation and appoints Edeeshia as the Guardian of Ben's person, and his daughter (Debbie) as the Guardian of his property. The arrangement doesn't work out. When Debbie refuses to pay for the health care decisions made by Edeeshia, the judge removes them as Guardians, and replaces them with a professional Guardian. The lesson to be learned from this story is more an observation:

> **A battle over who is to serve as Guardian**
> **is likely to follow, if a wealthy person**
> **neglects to take steps to avoid guardianship.**

You might think the simple solution is to have Ben sign a Durable Power of Attorney and a Health Care Directive. This story is more complicated than that. Ben is a wealthy businessman who is involved in several different business ventures. Avoiding guardianship for a man like Ben, requires a more advanced Estate Plan. At the very least, it requires a trust.

To rewrite this story to avoid guardianship we need to go back to a time before his accident.

I was attending a high society charitable ball. The party was organized to raise money for a local charity. I noticed Ben and Edeeshia Hooper as soon as they came into the ball room. How could you miss them? Edeeshia was a tall, dark skinned, head-turning beauty. Ben was a short, stocky, balding, almost pugnacious looking man. The photographer took their picture as they came into the room. Ben, being a very wealthy business man and Edeeshia as a former model, were used to such attention. Their picture appeared regularly in the society section of the newspaper.

Large round tables had been set up circling the dance floor. Name cards dictated the seating arrangement. I happened to be seated next to Ben. Dinner was noisy with waiters coming and going, people talking and the band playing. We didn't get much of a chance to talk, still Ben remembered me and the fact that I was a lawyer, because he came into my office some weeks later.

"Good to see you again, Ben. How is Edeeshia doing?"

"She's fine. She's at a spa close by, so I thought I'd come in and talk to you about a Will."

"A Will? Don't you have a trust?"

"No. I just want a simple Will. I don't have any patience for all that legal stuff."

He reached into his pocket and pulled out a cigar. He was about to llight up when I said, "This is a no smoking office Ben. Besides, you know smoking will stunt your growth."

He laughed, "We're going to get along just fine," he said as he returned the cigar to his pocket.

"Good." I answered, "Because we need to talk about what a Will can and can't do for you. A simple Will can't avoid probate. A Will can't avoid guardianship. The only thing a simple Will is good at doing is to distribute your property to your named beneficiaries. A man of your substance needs a more sophisticated Estate Plan — one that includes a trust."

Ben was not convinced, "We can do a trust later. Right now all I want is a Will."

With a man like Ben, it is important to flex muscles right away. I couldn't be his lawyer, if he didn't respect my legal opinion. "It would be malpractice for me to draft a simple Will for you. A Will doesn't nearly do all of the things you need to do to protect your property and provide for your health care in the event of your incapacity."

With that I got up out of my chair and said, "You'll need to find someone else to draft a Will for you."

Ben smiled and said, "You really feel strong about this, don't you? OK. Tell me about a trust."

THE TRUST

I returned to my chair and gave him my trust spiel, "A *Revocable Living Trust* is designed to care for your property during your lifetime, and then to distribute your property once you die — without the need for probate. To create a Revocable Living Trust, I will prepare a trust document (a *Trust Agreement*) designed to meet your needs. The Agreement is between the person who creates and funds the trust (the *Settlor* or *Grantor*) — that's you and the *Trustee* (the manager) of property placed in the trust — that's also you. The Settlor usually appoints himself as Trustee so that he is in total control of property he places into the trust. This means you will sign the Trust Agreement as the Settlor and also as the Trustee who promises to manage the property according to the terms of the Trust Agreement. The trust document also names a *Successor Trustee* who will take over the management of the trust property should the Trustee resign, become disabled, or die. Did you want Edeeshia to be your Successor Trustee?"

"No, no. She doesn't know anything about finances. It would have to be my brother, John."

We went on to discuss the beneficiaries of the trust. I noticed Edeeshia wasn't one of the beneficiaries. "As your wife, Edeeshia has legal rights to inherit your property, unless she signed away those rights.

"Yes, she did. We have a Premarital Agreement that gives her a million dollars after we're married ten years."

I recommended that he attach his Premarital Agreement to his Trust Agreement so that there would be no question as to Edeeshia's rights under the trust.

Ben still wasn't clear about how property got placed into and out of the trust. I explained, "Once your Trust Agreement is properly signed, you need to transfer your property into your trust. You do this by changing title from your individual name to your name as Trustee. For example, if you want to put a securities account into your trust, instruct your stockbroker to change the name on the account from Benjamin Hooper to:

BENJAMIN HOOPER , TRUSTEE OF THE BENJAMIN HOOPER REVOCABLE TRUST AGREEMENT.

When the change is made, all the securities in the account become trust property. You, wearing your Trustee hat, have total control of the account. You can take money out of and put money into the account, all as you see fit. If you want to put real property into your trust, I'll prepare a new deed with you the Grantor (and current owner), transferring the property to you as:

BENJAMIN HOOPER, TRUSTEE OF THE BENJAMIN HOOPER REVOCABLE TRUST AGREEMENT.

Once the transfer is made, it becomes trust property.

During your lifetime, you are free to *amend* (change the terms) your trust or even terminate (revoke) the trust altogether and have all your trust property placed back into your own name. If you do not revoke your trust during your lifetime, once you die the trust becomes irrevocable, and your Successor Trustee must follow the terms of the Trust Agreement as written. If the trust says to give the trust property to certain beneficiaries, your brother will do so, and without the need for probate. If your trust directs the Successor Trustee to hold property in trust and use the money to take care of a member of your family in the manner described in the Trust Agreement, then John will do so."

Once we completed our discussion of the trust, I recommended that he give his brother a Durable Power of Attorney.

Ben said "Why do I need a Power of Attorney if everything I own is in my trust?"

I explained "The Trustee of your trust only controls the property you place in your trust. If you become incapacitated, your Successor Trustee can't do personal things for you, like suing on your behalf or settling a claim that was filed against you or paying your personal taxes. Even if you have a trust, it is important to appoint an Attorney-In-Fact under a Durable Power of Attorney to do these important things for you, personally, in the event you can't."

I went onto a discussion of the importance of having a Health Care Directive.

Ben complained, "More documents? This is going to be one hell-of-a legal bill."

I smiled at him, "You're not telling me this Estate Plan is a financial stretch for you?"

He returned my smile sheepishly.

I explained the role of Health Care Agent and asked, "Did you want Edeeshia to be your Agent?"

"No. Make it my brother, Ben."

"Who do you want as an alternate?"

"That would be my daughter, Debbie."

We completed Ben's Estate Plan. I supervised the transfer of his property into his trust. We had a meeting with his brother John to explain the terms of the trust and his duties as Successor Trustee. John was so impressed with the many things that could be accomplished with a trust that he asked me to draft a trust for him as well.

Within the year Ben had the accident. John immediately took over the care of Ben's trust property. He also took charge of Ben's medical care. Edeeshia and Debbie had no problem with the arrangement. The accident left them in shock. They had no experience in making financial or medical decisions. They were content to have John in control. A few weeks later Edeeshia told John about "Stimulation Therapy" was being done on people who were in a coma. John said he would try anything to help his brother regain consciousness. He transferred Ben to the treatment center. The therapy did not bring Ben out of his coma. He died a few months later.

This story may not have a happy ending, however it did have a peaceful ending. There was no court battle over who was to serve as Guardian because there was no need to have a Guardian appointed. There was no squabble over how Ben's money should be spent while he was incapacitated. His Trust Agreement spelled it all out, and John followed the terms of the trust.

Because I represented Ben, and not Edeeshia, I never advised her to challenge the Premarital Agreement. She accepted the amount that she inherited under the Agreement. In addition to avoiding conservatorship, the trust avoided the need for probate. John distributed Ben's property according to the terms of the trust and the Premarital Agreement. Debbie and Edeeshia took their respective inheritances and went their separate ways.

Chapter 4 Rewrite

The Contested Capacity Hearing

Frank came down with ALS, a motor neuron disease that gradually destroys the neurons that control voluntary muscle activity (walking, writing, speaking, swallowing, breathing). Frank lived with his niece (Barbara), who saw to his everyday needs. As his illness progressed, she directed his medical care as well.

Frank had a long-time relationship with his financial advisor (Manny). Together they increased the size of Frank's portfolio to $800,000. As Frank's health declined Manny had Frank give him a Power of Attorney. When Barbara discovered that Frank allowed Manny to transfer all of Frank's securities to an account in Manny's name, she tried to have Frank declared incapacitated and in need of a Guardian.

Although the Court Investigator reported that Frank lacked capacity to handle his finances and make medical decisions, the judge was swayed by Frank's testimony and refused to appoint a Guardian. Manny knew that as Frank's illness progressed, it was just a matter of time before Barbara would be able to have herself appointed Guardian. Over the objections of Frank's family, Manny took Frank, and his $800,000, out of the country. They were never heard of again.

This case is hard to rewrite. After all, Frank did avoid guardianship — but was avoiding guardianship in Frank's best interest?

Frank did give someone a Durable Power of Attorney, however it was the wrong person. Frank never guessed that Manny would turn out to be untrustworthy. Frank knew Manny for such a long time, and they made all that money together.

Frank should have revoked that Power of Attorney as soon as he learned that Manny transferred Frank's property into Manny's name, however by then Frank's mind was slipping and he did not recognize the transfer as a dishonest act.

This is one of those cases where guardianship would have been a very good thing — regardless of the cost of establishing and maintaining the guardianship.

The only way to rewrite this story is to replace Judge Wecco with Judge Stone (the good judge described in Chapter 1 of this book). Judge Stone would also have been moved by Frank's tears. That wouldn't have stopped him from recognizing the need to protect Frank and his property. Judge Stone would have appointed Barbara as Guardian. He would have ordered Manny to transfer the funds to a guardianship account. Barbara would have continued to care for her uncle at home. Manny would not have been able whisk Frank out of the country. Of course without the money, Manny wouldn't want to do that anyway.

But this rewrite is just fantasy. The reality is that the court system let Frank, and his family, down.

The bad guy won.

Chapter 5 Rewrite

Avoiding Guardianship
For The Disabled

A single person (Arthur) comes down with Parkinson's. As the disease progresses, he has trouble keeping his apartment clean. He employs a house cleaner (Connie) to assist him. They have much in common. She's from Mexico as was his mother. Arthur soon becomes Connie's full time job. He buys a specially equipped car for his transportation, and puts the car in Connie's name. When Arthur's daughter (Isabella) learns of the gift she accuses Connie of exploitation and asks the state Department of Aging to investigate the matter. With my assistance, Arthur convinces the department that the charges are unfounded.

Eventually Arthur requires 24 hour care, however Connie has two small children and cannot leave them alone at night. They decide to buy a house large enough for all of them to live in. Arthur agrees to put the house in Connie's name in exchange for his lifetime care. Fearing another investigation, Arthur decides to keep a Life Estate for himself and give the Remainder Interest to Connie. I documented the closing to show that Arthur was of sound mind when he made the purchase.

Eventually Arthur requires skilled nursing care. When Isabella asks to become his Guardian, Connie wants to try to become Arthur's Guardian, however she fears that trying to become Guardian will expose her status as illegal alien.

Knowing that Arthur would not want his daughter to be his Guardian, I ask a charitable organization to serve as his professional Guardian, and the Court appoints it as Arthur's Guardian.

I later discover that the attorney for the charitable organization (Ed) is a prominent litigator. Ed asks the Court to allow him to file a lawsuit against Connie to recover the Remainder Interest on behalf of the Ward. During the course of the lawsuit Ed discovers Connie is an illegal alien. He alerts immigration and Connie is returned to Mexico. The lawsuit is eventually settled with Connie giving up all rights to the home. The Guardian sells the house to pay for Ed's fees and for the settlement as well.

This story shines a light on a flaw in the guardianship system. It is too easy to second guess transfers made by the Ward before he became incapacitated and then sue to recover the item "for the benefit of the Ward." Arthur already owned a Life Estate. It might benefit his daughter to recover the Remainder Interest — not Arthur. The true motive behind the lawsuit was to make money for the law firm representing the professional Guardian — a sort of pay-back by the charitable organization to the lawyer for contributing his time and money to that worthy cause.

The problem is the system itself. The way to correct the problem is to pass a law requiring that before a lawsuit is filed "on behalf of the Ward," the Guardian needs to prove to the Court that there is probable cause for wrong-doing and that the lawsuit is in the best interest of the Ward. The standard of proof should be by clear and convincing evidence.

In other words, state law should require that before allowing a Guardian to sue, a probable cause hearing be held. The Guardian would be required to prove that some wrongdoing took place resulting in harm to the Ward <u>and</u> that the lawsuit will profit the Ward. The judge could not allow the lawsuit unless he was very sure that the Guardian had proved his case.

If there were such a law, Connie would have had an opportunity to explain to the Court the circumstances of the transfer. I would have had an opportunity to play the videotape showing that Arthur knew exactly what he was doing when he gave Connie the Remainder Interest. Hopefully, the Court would have found there was no probable cause to support a finding of wrongdoing.

If that were not enough to stop the lawsuit, the second statutory requirement should do so — namely, the Guardian would need to prove to the Court that suing to regain the Remainder Interest would be in the best interest of the Ward. The only one to profit from the lawsuit (besides the lawyer) would be Isabella. Arthur already owned the Life Estate interest in the home. Taking the Remainder Interest away from Connie would result in Arthur owing the Life Estate and the Remainder Interest. Upon his death, the Remainder Interest would go Isabella instead of Connie. It was in Isabella's best interest to sue — not Arthur's.

As of the year 2009, this author knows of no such law in any state. In fact, in several states, a Guardian can sue without asking Court permission to do so. This being the case, we need to rewrite this story to avoid guardianship in the first place. To do that we need to go back to the time Arthur closed on the house.

THE PRENEED GUARDIAN

Once the closing was over, I explained to Arthur, "We've done as much as we can to show that you freely, and with full understanding, gave Connie a Remainder Interest in your home. This doesn't guarantee that Isabella won't try to challenge the gift. Her complaint to the Department of Aging may not have been successful, however she can still tell a judge that you don't know what you're doing and ask to be appointed as your Guardian."

Arthur asked, "How can she do that? I don't need a Guardian. I can take care of myself."

"Yes, still you need to keep in mind that Parkinson's is a progressive disease. Unless there is a medical breakthrough, eventually you will become incapacitated."

Arthur was upset, "I absolutely don't want Isabella to be my Guardian. I want Connie to take care of me."

"One way to head off guardianship is to give Connie authority to take care of your finances with a Durable Power of Attorney. Connie can use the Power of Attorney to pay your bills if you later become incapacitated. You can sign a Health Care Directive appointing Connie as your Health Care Agent to make your medical decisions should you become too ill to do so yourself."

"Will that guarantee Isabella will never be my Guardian?"

"It should. However, if you become incapacitated, Isabella might be able to convince a judge that Connie has been taking advantage of you. The judge might decide to make Isabella your Guardian. Maybe the better route to go is to assume you are going to need a Guardian and take steps to have Connie appointed as your Guardian."

Arthur asked, "How do we do that?."

I explained, "You can have a Guardian appointed right now. You have a progressive disease. As it is you cannot walk on your own. In time, you won't be able to take care of yourself at all. I'm sure the judge will have no problem appointing the person of your choice to care for you."

Arthur said, "OK. Let's do the Health Care Directive, and the Power of Attorney and get Connie appointed as my Guardian."

I called Connie back into the room. I explained what Arthur wanted to do. She was seemed hesitant when we discussed the guardianship. "You mean I have to go to Court?"

"Yes. What's the problem?"

Connie asked, "Will they check my background?"

"Many states have laws require a background check before appointing someone to be Guardian. This state doesn't have such a law at this time."

Connie worried, "They could pass such a law, couldn't they?"

"Sure. Why are you so worried about a background check?"

Then it all came out — how Connie entered the country so many years before as an illegal alien. She feared the police and the court system. "No, I can't take a chance on becoming Arthur's Guardian."

I suggested to Arthur, "Connie can't be your Guardian, however, you can employ a professional Guardians. I can recommend Nancy Williams. I worked with her on other cases. She does a great job. You could ask her to be your Guardian. You can tell her you want to remain in your home with Connie caring for you as long as possible."

Arthur didn't mind having Connie as his Guardian, but not anyone else, "If Nancy is my Guardian, she'll be the one to decide if I stay at home or go to a nursing home. I'm not ready to let someone make that decision for me."

I offered another suggestion, "You could appoint Nancy as your *Preneed Guardian*."

"What's a Preneed Guardian?" asked Arthur.

"A competent adult can name a Preneed Guardian to take over as his Guardian if and when he is determined by a Court to be in need of a Guardian. I can draft a *Declaration Of Preneed Guardian* naming Nancy as your choice of Guardian. If Isabella ever asks to be appointed as your Guardian, your choice of Guardian will have priority."

Arthur followed my advice and appointed Nancy as his Preneed Guardian.

Some time later Arthur had to go into a nursing home. Isabella filed a petition to be appointed as Guardian of her father. She withdrew the petition when she found out that her father had appointed a Preneed Guardian, so no one was ever appointed as Arthur's Guardian.

With the Durable Power of Attorney and Health Care Directive, Connie was able to care for Arthur until he died.

Isabella never learned about the Life Estate until after her father died. When Isabella found out that Connie now owned her father's home she consulted with an attorney.

My name was on the deed as the attorney who prepared the deed with the Life Estate Interest, so the attorney called me. I told him about the video tape and all of the precautions we took to ensure that there would be no question about Arthur's capacity or of undue influence. I invited him to my office to view the tape. He took me up on the offer within the week.

He must have advised Isabella not to pursue the matter because neither I, nor Connie, ever heard from Isabella again.

So far as I know, Connie and her children are still living in the house Arthur purchased for them.

Chapter 6 Rewrite

The Developmentally Disabled Adult

Janet (age 43) discovers she is pregnant. Her husband (Kenneth (age 52) is upset by the news. They already have two girls, Victoria (age 11) and Ellen (age 8). He does not want to raise children into his old age. He urges his wife to seek an abortion. She will hear none of it.

Although Kenneth, Jr. is born prematurely, doctors assure the couple that he will be just fine. Kenny seemed to develop normally, however by his third birthday, Janet is concerned that something is wrong. It isn't until Kenny's fifth birthday that he is diagnosed with autism and epilepsy. The news is more than his father can handle. Kenneth not only divorces Janet, he, in effect, divorces his son by giving up all custodial rights to the child. As part of the divorce settlement, he is required to pay alimony to Janet for fifteen years and to set up a trust to provide lifetime care for his son's special needs.

Once divorced, it is up to Janet to raise her three children. A disproportionate amount of her time is spent caring for Kenny. She becomes actively involved in promoting research for the treatment and care of the developmentally disabled.

The years pass. Victoria and Ellen go off on their own. Ellen marries and raises a family. Victoria never seems to settle down, going job to job, town to town.

As Janet ages she thinks of what will happen to Kenny should she die, however she doesn't dwell on it. She knows that the trust fund is more than enough to provide for Kenny's support. She figures that one of his sisters will take him in and provide for his custodial care.

WRONG!

When it comes to a developmentally disabled child, a parent needs to make firm plans for the financial support of the child and for his custodial care as well.

Janet should have seen the warning signs. Ellen had her hands full raising twin boys. She could barely manage her own family, none the less take on the care of her man/child brother. Victoria was not a stable person. How could Kenny possibly fit into Victoria's rolling stone life style?

And why would either sister want to take responsibility for their brother? Didn't Janet notice that there was little affection between Ellen and her brother — and absolutely no relationship between Victoria and her brother?

Janet sure had a blind spot when it came to her children. That blind spot cost Kenny months of abuse. It could have cost him his life.

To give this story a happy ending we need to go back to when Janet was 60 years old and was beginning to think about what would happen to Kenny if she become disabled or die. We need to give her 20/20 emotional vision. She needs to see her children as they really are — not as she would like them to be. She needs to recognize the importance of taking legal steps to provide for Kenny's care.

THE STANDBY GUARDIAN

Janet at 60 looked older than her years. When she told me her story I realized those wrinkles were a result of a very hard life. Yet she didn't think of her life as being hard. "Kenny may be disabled, still he's been a joy to me. I just worry about who will care for him once I'm gone."

"You said that Ellen lives near by. Do you think she would be able to take Kenny into her home and care for him?"

Janet laughed, "Heavens no. She has 18 month old twins. She can barely take care of them."

I asked, "What about Victoria?

"No. She's not close to her brother, and besides she likes to travel around. I couldn't imagine her wanting to be responsible for him. No. I can't think of any family member that would be able to take him into their home. Couldn't he stay where he is and have someone come in to care for him?"

I didn't think her plan was realistic, "Kenny needs 24 hour care. That means he'll need three shifts of caretakers coming in each day. That's expensive. From what I can see from his trust, it isn't designed to provide such care. Kenny is 16. He may need care for the rest of his life. That could be a long time."

Janet was concerned, "I could place Kenny in a group home, but I want him to stay with me for as long as I am able to care for him. The only problem is how to arrange for his care if I die suddenly."

I suggested she look for a group home and work out an arrangement so that he stays at the group home for short periods of time. "Once you see that he is happy in that environment, you can gradually increase the time he spends there. Should you die suddenly, the transition to group living will be much easier on Kenny. Getting some time for yourself should be another plus."

Janet was concerned about who would have the authority to place Kenny in the group home once she died and who would have authority to use the funds from Kenny's trust for his benefit.

I explained, "Kenny will need a Guardian to care for his person and for his property. You could put a provision in your Will naming someone to serve as Kenny's Guardian. There are three roadblocks to that approach. First, your Will needs to be admitted to probate and accepted by the Court as being valid. Second, a judge must determine that Kenny is disabled and in need of a Guardian. Finally, the judge needs to agree that appointing your choice of Guardian is best for Kenny."

Janet saw the problem. "That approach may take several weeks, and there's no guarantee that the judge will appoint my choice of Guardian."

I suggested a better route, "As the parent of a developmentally disabled child, you can ask the Court to appoint you as Guardian, and the person of your choice as an alternate or [2] *Standby Guardian*. The Standby Guardian will take over should you become incapacitated or die."

[2] In some states, the judge appoints the parent and another as Co-Guardians. Should one person die or become disabled, the remaining person will serve as Guardian.

I explained, "This solves all three problems. Your Will doesn't need to accepted into probate in order to have Ellen appointed as Kenny's Guardian. When we apply for a Standby Guardian, the Court will determine that Kenny is in need of a Guardian, so there will be no delay waiting for a Court Investigator to examine Kenny once you are deceased. The best part is that your choice of Guardian is approved by the Court."

Janet agreed, "Let's have Ellen appointed as Standby Guardian. I'll line up a group home and tell Ellen that should anything happen to me, Kenny is to live at the group home.

And that is what we did.

Nine years later Janet died. As Standby Guardian, Ellen immediately assumed responsibility for Kenny's care. He had been living at the group home during the week and with his mother on weekends, so the transition to full time group living was not hard for him.

Ellen and Victoria inherited Janet's home. They sold the house. Each took half of the proceeds, and once again Victoria took off for parts unknown.

Chapter 7 Rewrite

Controlling The Guardianship
Of A Minor

Large sums of money and an unprotected minor or incapacitated person are an open invitation to predators of the human kind. By unprotected, we mean that no one thought ahead to provide for the financial care and physical well being of the minor or incapacitated person. One such example was given in Chapter 3. Ben Hooper was a wealthy businessman. When he became incapacitated, his wife, child, and brother all fought to control his fortune. We saw it again in Chapter 6. All Victoria wanted was to access to Kenny's trust to support her drug habit. That chapter was appropriately titled *Guardian Devil.*

Chapter 7 is more of the same. When their mother (Cathy) is killed in a car accident, her children (Tammy and Jimmy) are awarded millions of dollars it the settlement of a lawsuit for her wrongful death. Her former husband (James) and his mother each want to be Guardian. Tammy thwarts those plans by putting on an act in court. Her caring grandmother (Lorraine) is appointed Guardian. James and his mother go back to what they were doing before Cathy was killed — living their lives without any interest in the children.

This story had a happy, albeit sad, ending — yet it was close. The judge almost appointed the children's abusive, alcoholic, father as their Guardian. It could have been another Guardian Devil situation. So how does a parent protect his child from guardianship?

Probably, not at all. There are few ways to avoid guardianship, if a minor is awarded a large sum of money as a result of a lawsuit, or an inheritance, or as the beneficiary of insurance proceeds. In most states, a transfer of funds to a minor that exceeds $10,000 must be approved by a Court. If the sum being transferred is significant, the judge will appoint a Guardian to care for the property until the child is an adult.

The Court usually appoints the parent as Guardian. The parent manages the property under the supervision of the Court. The parent needs to account to the Court each year. James being an irresponsible, if not dishonest, parent could have done some serious mischief with the money during that time. However, the real danger in this story was James taking physical custody of the children. What a hellish childhood they would have had to endure under the control of their dead-beat father.

A parent may not be able to avoid guardianship for his minor child and probably would not want to do so, even if he could. Most parents welcome Court supervision of whomever is taking care of their child in the event the parent is not there to care for the child. What the parent really wants is to control the choice of Guardian.

How do you ensure that a Guardian Angel will be there for your children should you become disabled or die? First you need to be able to recognize the difference between the good guys and the bad guys. That was the problem with Cathy from the beginning. Even after the divorce she thought of James as a good father and agreed to joint custody of the children. Cathy couldn't take steps to terminate the parental rights of her husband until she woke up to the fact of his abusive nature.

Lorraine knew there was no point in telling Cathy that she should either enforce the child support order or terminate James' parental rights. Cathy never listened to her mother when James was being most abusive. Why would she pay any attention now that James was no longer in her life?

No. It will take the kiss of a Prince Charming to wake up this sleeping beauty.

Prince Charming came in the form of the new cook who was hired at the restaurant where Cathy worked. Cathy didn't think of Mike as a Prince Charming. He wasn't good looking. He was slightly balding, and on the heavy side. Whatever he lacked in looks, he made up in personality. He was always cheerful, often singing as he cooked, making jokes and openly flirting with Cathy. The other waitresses encouraged her to go out with Mike. Cathy resisted saying he wasn't her type. When she told Lorraine about Mike, her mother agreed he wasn't Cathy's type. "Your type is the 'put me down,' 'insult me,' 'take advantage of me,' 'control me,' type of guy. You wouldn't know what to do with a guy who is hard-working, good-natured, and treats you with respect."

Cathy didn't appreciate the sarcasm, still she knew there was some truth in what her mother was saying. She thought about those words when Mike sent her a dozen roses for her birthday and four tickets for her and her Mom to take the children to an ice show. Lorraine didn't want to go to the show, "I've seen ice shows before. You seen 'em one, you seen 'em all. See if Mike won't go in my place."

Cathy knew exactly what her mother was doing — still Mike was such a nice guy and so much fun to be around, she agreed to go with him and the kids.

The outing became the first of many. The kids loved Mike and he loved them, and of course he loved Cathy.

Mike always wanted children. He pictured himself as having a large family — yet at 37, he was still a single man. He thought this ready-made family was just the one for him — as a starter. He wanted more children. Cathy wasn't sure that was a good idea. "I don't want it to be *my* children and *our* children. My children might become second class children."

Mike protested, "I think of them as my children right now — even without us being married. I would love to adopt them as soon as we marry."

Which is how I came to meet Cathy, Mike and Lorraine. They all came to my office asking whether there was a chance that Mike could adopt the children after the marriage. I explained to Cathy, "When a couple divorce, whoever is given custody of the child is considered to be the child's natural Guardian. That means the custodial parent is the Guardian of the personal needs of the child and of the property of the child. By agreeing to joint custody, you allowed James to keep his parental rights. Those rights either need to be terminated by a Court, or James will need to agree to the adoption.

Lorraine didn't think that would work. "Jim doesn't want to be father, but he would never agree to someone else being father."

Cathy agreed, "I haven't seen or heard from him in years. He never once called or came to see the children. He never paid child support. Still I don't think he would want to give up his rights."

I said, "You need to remind James that along with rights comes responsibilities. If he doesn't want to give up his rights, he needs to start making child support payments AND he needs to pay you for all of the back child support."

Cathy called a few days later. She located James. He was still living in Las Vegas. He had remarried and had a six month old baby girl.

Cathy was angry as she told me about the conversation, "Jim told me he hadn't had a drink in two years. He said he thought that the reason he drank was because I made him so unhappy. I couldn't believe he said that. I never cheated on him. I gave him every penny I earned. I never did anything wrong. How could <u>he</u> be the unhappy one?"

I said, "I've never seen a divorce that didn't involve two unhappy people. You were both lucky to go your separate ways. What about the adoption? Will he give up his parental rights?"

"He sure will. I didn't even have to threaten him with back child support."

I filed a petition to terminate parental rights pending adoption. James joined in the petition asking that his parental rights be terminated. Mike signed the petition, saying that he wanted to adopt the children as soon as the couple married. The judge granted the petition and terminated Jim's parental rights. The adoption hearing was scheduled for the following month as soon as the couple returned from their honeymoon in Hawaii.

PRENEED GUARDIAN OF A MINOR

After the hearing I suggested that Cathy make provision for the care of the children in her absence, "Hawaii's a long way off. It's a good idea to appoint your mother as the Preneed Guardian of the children. It's easy to do. I'll draft a *Declaration Of Preneed Guardian* appointing your mother as Guardian, to take effect upon your death or incapacity. State law requires both parents to appoint a Preneed Guardian, however now that Jim's parental rights are terminated, it only takes your signature."

Cathy said, "I thought people did that as part of their Will."

"Yes. That's another way to appoint a Guardian for your children. Did you want me to draft a Will for you?"

"No. There's too much going on in my life right now. I'll just appoint a Preneed Guardian."

Luckily Cathy heeded my advice because a few days later she was hit by a Hummer and died. Lorraine took over the care of the children. Right after the funeral, we filed a petition to have Lorraine appointed as Guardian. I attached the Declaration to the petition. There was no battle for guardianship because James terminated his parental rights.

Mike never did get a chance to adopt the children, yet he stayed in their lives — visiting for the holidays and special occasions. Lorraine said he was the son she never had. Soon they were calling him Uncle Mike. That relationship became all the more important to the children when Lorraine died. By then Tammy was a grown woman. Jimmy at 18 still needed the guidance of a father figure, and Mike was just the man for the job.

Afterthoughts

Sending a book off to the publisher is always difficult for me. I read the book through, cover to cover, at least two times. I try to put myself in the shoes of the reader. Will he find the book interesting or will he find me guilty of the cardinal writer crime of boredom?

With this book, I was also worried about whether I got the message of the importance of avoiding guardianship across. As I did my review, I became concerned. I wasn't too sure whether some readers might think, "Guardianship isn't all that bad. It was the judge who caused all the trouble."

Lest there be any such misconception — most judges do a decent job. They are honest, hard working and conscientious. A few top judges do an outstanding job. At the other end of the scale are those judges who may be lazy or incompetent, if not corrupt.

The reason four of the seven cases I described were decisions by a lower-end judge was explained in the book. There is only one judge in our county who presides over guardianship matters. That judge is rotated every five years. The presiding judge may have been in that small percentage of judges at the low end of the scale, however because he was the only guardianship judge in our county, I had to practice before him 100% of the time during that five year period. Hence the skewed result of four bad decisions out of seven cases. Still, good judge or bad, once you become involved in a guardianship, as a Guardian or a Ward, you are no longer in charge of your destiny and that's what is wrong with guardianship.

CONTROLLING YOUR DESTINY

In the Introduction to this book, I spoke of how a book written by Norman Dacey changed the way people thought of probate. Up to that time, most were happy to go through probate because it meant that they were about to inherit money. Dacey's book brought to the attention of the general public, that probate is an unnecessary expense and one that can be avoided. The purpose of this book is to create a similar public perception of guardianship. Guardianship is not only an unnecessary expense, it is the surrender of your legal rights to someone who may not always have your best interest at heart.

It is easier to avoid guardianship than it is to avoid probate. For the healthy adult it just involves giving a trusted family member a Durable Power of Attorney for finances and appointing someone to serve as his Health Care Agent. Avoiding guardianship for the disabled child or adult may take the assistance of an attorney.

It is important to prepare for disability— regardless of how remote you may think the chances of ever needing a Guardian may be.

It's like fire insurance. The vast majority of us will never experience a house fire, still we purchase house insurance every year — just in case. Preparing for your incapacity (or for a loved one) is insurance that a judge (good or bad) never gets to decide who should care for you (or your loved one) because you took steps to avoid guardianship.

Glossary

ACTUARIAL TABLE An *actuarial table* is a table organized according to statistical data that indicates the life expectancy of a person.

ADMINISTRATION The *administration* of a probate estate is the management and settlement of the decedent's affairs. There are different types of administration. See **SUMMARY ADMINISTRATION.**

AFFIDAVIT An *Affidavit* is a written statement of fact made by someone (the *Affiant*) voluntarily, under oath, or acknowledged as being true, in the presence of a notary public or someone else who has authority to administer an oath or take acknowledgments.

AGENT An *Agent* is someone who is authorized by another (the *principal)* to act for or in place of the principal.

ALIMONY *Alimony* is an allowance which someone is required by Court order to pay to his /her spouse. The allowance is for the spouse's support while they are separated or after their divorce.

ALS *ALS* is the abbreviation for Amyotrophic Lateral Sclerosis, a motor neuron disease. It is also known as Lou Gerhrig's disease, after the famous baseball player.

ALZHEIMER'S DISEASE *Alzheimer's Disease* is a degenerative brain disease. It causes progressive memory loss, impaired thinking, disorientation, and changes in personality and mood.

AMENDMENT   An *amendment* to a Trust is an addition to the Trust that changes the provisions of the Trust.

ASSET An *asset* is anything owned by someone that has a value, including personal property (jewelry, paintings, securities, cash, motor vehicles, etc.) and real property (condominiums, vacant lots, acreage, residences, etc.).

ATTORNEY or ATTORNEY AT LAW An *attorney*, also known as an *Attorney at law*, or a *lawyer*, is someone who is licensed by the state to practice law in that state.

ATTORNEY-IN-FACT An *Attorney-In-Fact* is someone appointed to act as an Agent for another (the *Principal*) under a Power of Attorney.

AUDIT An *Audit* is a systematic financial review using generally accepted accounting principals.

BALIFF A Court *Baliff* is an officer of the court who is in charge of keeping order while the court is in session.

BENEFICIARY A *beneficiary* is one who benefits from the act of another or from the transfer of property. In this book we refer to a beneficiary as someone named in a Will, Trust, or deed to receive property, or someone who inherits property under the Laws of Intestate Succession.

BEYOND A REASONABLE DOUBT *Beyond A Reasonable Doubt* is a standard of proof used in criminal cases. It means to be fully satisfied and entirely convinced.

BURDEN OF PROOF The *burden of proof* is the duty of one of the parties in a dispute to establish the facts in the case. Who has the burden of proof is established by law.

CASE LAW *Case Law* refers to decisions made by an Appeal Court using the same or similar set of circumstances. Case Law sets a precedent that other judges can use to decide the case before them.

CLEAR AND CONVINCING EVIDENCE *Clear and convincing evidence* is less than the criminal standard of *beyond a reasonable doubt*, but greater than the civil suit standard of *by a preponderance* of the evidence.

CONFLICT OF INTEREST A *conflict of interest* is a conflict between the official duties of a fiduciary (guardian, Trustee, attorney, etc.) and his own private interest. For example, it is a conflict of interest for a Successor Trustee to use Trust property for his own personal profit.

CO-PERSONAL REPRESENTATIVE
See **PERSONAL REPRESENTATIVE**

CONTINGENCY FEE AGREEMENT A *Contingency Fee Agreement* is an agreement between attorney and client whereby the attorney works for a percentage of the amount recovered, e.g. 30% of the amount awarded to the client in the law suit. This type of fee agreement is frequently used in personal injury cases.

COURT The word *Court* is used two ways. Court, spelled with small letter "c," refers to a physical place, i.e., the court house or the court room. Court with a capital "c," is synonymous with "judge," i.e., an "order of the Court" is an order made by the judge of the court.

COURT INVESTIGATOR A *Court Investigate* is person appointed by the Court, to investigate and then report back to the Court about a matter that is before the Court.

C-SECTION *C-Section* is the abbreviation for a *Caesarean Section*, a surgical method of delivering a baby.

DAMAGES *Damages* is money that is awarded by a Court as compensation to someone who has been injured by the action of another.

DISCOVERY *Discovery* is the pre-trial methods used by opposing parties to obtain facts and information about the case. See DEPOSITION.

DISTRIBUTION The *distribution* of a Trust or Probate Estate is the giving to the beneficiary that part of the Estate to which the beneficiary is entitled.

DURABLE As used in the Power of Attorney, the word *durable* means that the Power of Attorney will remain in effect in the event that the principal (the person giving the Power of Attorney) becomes incapacitated.

DURESS *Duress* is the use of force or threats to get someone to do something.

ESTATE A person's *Estate* is all of the property (both real and personal property) owned by that person. The guardianship Estate is all of the property owned by the Ward that is under the management and control of his Guardian.

FAMILY COURT The *Family Court* is that division of the Court that deals with adoption, divorce, separation, paternity, support and child care.

GERONTOLOGIST A *Gerontologist* is a professional who specializes in the aging process and the problems associated with aging.

GRANTEE The *Grantee* of a deed is the person who receives title to real property from the *Grantor*.

GRANTOR A *Grantor* is someone who transfers property. The Grantor of a deed, is the person who transfers real property to a new owner (the *Grantee*). The Grantor of a Trust is someone who creates the Trust and then transfers property into the Trust. See SETTLOR.

GROUP HOME A *Group Home* is a housing unit designed to care for a group of persons who, because of some mental or physical disability, need 24 hour supervision.

GUARDIAN A *Guardian* is a person appointed by the Court to care for the person or the property of someone (the *Ward*) who is a minor or who has been determined by the Court to be incapacitated. In some states, a Guardian is referred to as a *Conservator* and the Ward is called the *Conservatee.*

GUARDIAN AD LITEM A *Guardian Ad Litem* is a person appointed by the Court to represent the best interests of the Ward in a legal matter that is pending before the Court.

HEALTH CARE AGENT A *Health Care Agent* is someone who is appointed by another (the *Principal)* to authorize medical treatment for the Principal, in the event he is to too ill to do so himself.

HEALTH CARE DIRECTIVE A *Health Care Directive* is a writing made by someone (the *declarant*) in which the declarant gives directions about the health care he/she wishes to receive in the event he is too ill to direct his own treatment. The document generally includes a LIVING WILL and the appointment of a HEALTH CARE AGENT. In some states, the document is called an *Advance Health Care Directive*, or a *Health Care Proxy*, or a *Health Care Power of Attorney*.

HEIR   An *Heir* is anyone entitled to inherit the decedent's property under the Laws of Intestate Succession in the event that the decedent dies without a valid Will.

HOMESTEAD The *homestead* is the dwelling that is owned, and occupied, as the owner's principal residence.

INCAPACITATED The term *incapacitated* is used in two ways. A person is *physically incapacitated*, if he lacks the ability to perform certain tasks. A person is *legally incapacitated*, if a Court finds that he is unable to care for his person or property.

IRREVOCABLE TRUST An *Irrevocable Trust* is a Trust that cannot be changed, cancelled or terminated until its purpose is accomplished.

LAWS OF INTESTATE SUCCESSION The *Laws of Intestate Succession* are the laws of the state that determine who inherits the decedent's Probate Estate, and how much he inherits, in the event that the decedent died without a valid Will. In some states, these laws are called the *Laws of Descent and Distribution*.

LIMITED GUARDIAN A *Limited Guardian* is someone appointed by the Court to exercise only those legal rights specifically designed to meet the needs of a person, after the Court determines that person lacks the capacity to do some, but not all of the tasks necessary to care for his person or property.

LIVING WILL   A *Living Will* is a Health Care Advance Directive that gives instructions to the physician about whether life support systems should be withheld or withdrawn in the event the *Declarant* (the person who made the Living Will) is terminally ill, or in a persistent vegetative state, and unable to speak for himself.

MEDICAID *Medicaid* is a medical assistance program sponsored jointly by the federal and state government to provide health care for people with low income and limited resources.

MEMORANDUM OF LAW A *Memorandum Of Law* is a writing submitted to the Court to support a position taken by one of the parties. It contains a statement of the law as written as well as cases decided by a court of law that support the argument being presented.

NET WORTH A person's *net worth* is the fair market value of all of the property that he owns less the sum of his liabilities, i.e. what he owes.

NEXT OF KIN *Next of kin* refers to a person's nearest blood relation or it can refer to those people (not necessarily blood relations) who are entitled to inherit the property of a person under the Laws of Intestate Succession.

PERSONAL PROPERTY *Personal property* is all property owned by a person that is not real property (real estate). It includes personal effects, cars, securities, bank accounts, insurance policies, etc.

PERSONAL REPRESENTATIVE The *Personal Representative* is someone appointed by the Probate Court to settle the decedent's Estate and to distribute whatever is left to the proper beneficiary. If two people are appointed, they serve as *Co-Personal Representatives*. In general, Co-Personal Representatives have equal authority, and the signatures of both are required on all transactions.

PREMARITAL AGREEMENT A *Premarital Agreement* (also known as an *Antenuptial* or a *Prenuptial Agreement*) is an Agreement made prior to marriage to take effect once a couple marry. The Agreement states how the couple's property is to be managed during their marriage and how their property is to be divided should either die, or they later divorce.

PREPONDERANCE OF THE EVIDENCE A *Preponderance of the Evidence* is a standard of proof used in civil trials. It is evidence that is more convincing than the evidence offered in opposition.

PRINCIPAL OF A POWER OF ATTORNEY The *Principal* of a Power of Attorney is someone who gives another (his *Agent*) authority to act on his (the Principal's) behalf.

PRINCIPAL OF A TRUST The *Principal of a Trust* is the Trust property. The Trust income is the money that is earned on the Trust Principal.

PROBABLE CAUSE *Probable cause* exists if it is reasonable to believe certain facts. Mere suspicion is not enough. For probable cause to exist, there must be more evidence for the facts than against.

PROBATE *Probate* is a Court procedure in which a Court determines the existence of a valid Will. The decedent's Estate is then settled by the Personal Representative who pays all valid claims and then distributes whatever remains to the proper beneficiary.

PROBATE ESTATE The *Probate Estate* is that part of the decedent's Estate that is subject to a Probate procedure. It includes property that the decedent owned in his name.

PRO BONO The term *Pro Bono* means "for the public good." When an attorney works Pro Bono, he does so voluntarily and without pay.

PROFESSIONAL GUARDIAN A *Professional Guardian* is a person, or business entity, who is the Court appointed Guardian of two or more Wards, at the same time, who are not related to the Ward through blood or marriage. Requirements to become a Professional Guardian vary significantly state to state, from no state license or background check, to state licensing complete with educational requirements and testing and a thorough FBI background check.

PUBLIC GUARDIAN A *Public Guardian* is an individual or business entity appointed by the Court to serve as Guardian for an incapacitated person who is unable to pay for a Professional Guardian and who has no family member or friend who is willing or able to serve as Guardian.

QUIT CLAIM DEED See WARRANTY DEED

RETAINER In law, when a client employs an attorney, he is said to have retained the attorney. The act of employment is called the *retainer*.

REVERSE MORTGAGE A *Reverse Mortgage* a mortgage in which the mortgage loan proceeds are disbursed periodically to the borrower. The loan is generally repaid in a lump sum when the borrower dies or the property is sold.

SETTLOR A *Settlor* or a *Trustor* is someone who creates a Trust.

SPRINGING POWER OF ATTORNEY A *Springing Power of Attorney* is a Power of Attorney that is not operational until, and unless, the Principal is incapacitated.

SSI *SSI* Is the abbreviation for *Supplemental Security Income*, a federal benefit given to qualified disabled persons.

STANDBY GUARDIAN A *Standby Guardian* is someone appointed by a parent to take over the care of a child in the event that the parent becomes incapacitated or dies.

SUCCESSOR TRUSTEE   A *Successor Trustee* is someone who takes the place of the Trustee.

SUMMARY ADMINISTRATION   A *Summary Administration* is a simplified and/or shortened Probate procedure.

SUPPORTED LIVING *Supported Living*, also referred to as a *Half Way House* is a housing unit for a group of people who need some (but not 24 hour) assistance with their everyday living.

TRUST AGREEMENT A *Trust Agreement* is a document in which someone (the *Settlor* or *Trustor*) creates a Trust and appoints a person or business entity (a *Trustee*) to manage property placed into the Trust.

UNDUE INFLUENCE *Undue influence* is pressure, influence or persuasion that overpowers a person's free will or judgment, so that a person acts according to the will or purpose of the dominating party.

VOLUNTARY GUARDIANSHIP A Court can appoint a Guardian of the property without a finding that the Ward is incapacitated. This type of guardianship is called a *Voluntary Guardianship* because the ward is free to terminate the guardianship at any time.

WARD A *Ward* is a person placed by the Court under the care and supervision of a Guardian.

WARRANTY DEED A *Warranty Deed* is a deed in which the Grantor warrants (promises) that the property he is transferring has good and clear title; i.e., that no one else has rights in the property. This is different than a *Quit-claim Deed* where the Grantor says, in effect, "I am releasing any interest I have in this property to you, but I make no guarantees about anyone else's right to this property."

WAIVER A *waiver* is the intentional and voluntary giving up of a known right.

WRONGFUL DEATH A *wrongful death* is a death that was caused by the willful or negligent act of a person or company.

Guardian Angel   Guardian Devil

INDEX

233

Other books by Amelia E. Pohl
Guiding Those Left Behind

Amelia E. Pohl has written a book explaining how to settle the affairs of someone you love.

- ✧ what agencies need to be notified
- ✧ how to locate the decedent's property
- ✧ what bills do and do not need to be paid
- ✧ how to get possession of the inheritance
- ✧ when you do, and do not, need an attorney
- ✧ the rights of a beneficiary, and much more.

As with this Will book, the Guiding book is designed for the average reader. Legal terminology has been kept to a minimum. There is a glossary at the end of the book in the event you come across a legal term not familiar to you.

BOOK REVIEWS OF *Guiding Those Left Behind*

ARIZONA

Ben T. Traywick of the Tombstone Epitaph said "This book is an excellent reference book that simplifies all the necessary tasks that must be done when there is a death in the family. There is even an explanation as to how you can arrange your own estate so that your heirs will not be left with a multitude of nagging problems." "The reviewer has been going through probate for two years with no end yet in sight. This book at the beginning two year ago would have helped immensely."

CALIFORNIA

Margot Petit Nichols of the Carmel Pine Cone called it a ". . . TRULY RIVETING READ." " . . . I could scarcely put it down." "This is a book that we should all have, either on our book shelves or thoughtfully placed with our important papers."

How To Defend Yourself Against Your Lawyer

is a book about the unhappy experiences people have with their lawyers, beginning with that of the author AMELIA E. POHL. She became involved in a law suit and found herself in the role of client, rather than lawyer. She become concerned about lawyers who do not provide their clients with loyalty and respect. This book is a result of those concerns.

The book is divided into chapters that cover the most common problems that take people to a lawyer: divorce, probate, criminal, personal injury, starting a business, making a Will, buying a house, etc. Each chapter tells of the misadventures of the unwary as they sought the services of a lawyer without a clue as to what they were "buying." This book is funny, sad, interesting, but most of all informative. It tells the reader how to become a savvy consumer, i.e., how to find the right lawyer for the right job. If you ever find the need to employ a lawyer, you will be glad you read this book.

Copyright 2004   274 pages   6" X 9"   soft cover
$20 includes Shipping and Handling

BOOK REVIEW

TED KREITER of the SATURDAY EVENING POST wrote:

"Horror fans, forget about those tawdry tales of ghosts and vampires. Pick up Amelia E. Pohl's *How To Defend Yourself Against Your Lawyer* to read some really scary stuff. Like the story . . . of the grieving widow, Ethel, whose husband died shortly after a lawyer drafted a sweetheart will for the two of them. . . . Six months in attorney's fees later, Ethel learned that she already had her husband's money because it never needed to go through probate! . . . Ethel then went out and found a lawyer for $1,000 who was able to get her $5,000 back. You do the math. . .

Following Pohl's useful advice could save a person much more than money."

A Will Is Not Enough

Many people who have a Will think that they have their affairs in order. They believe that their Will can take care of any problem that may arise. But the primary function of a Will is to distribute property to people named in a Will. A Will cannot:

⇨   Protect your assets and limit your debt

⇨   Provide care for a minor or disabled child

⇨   Appoint someone to make your health care decisions should you be unable to do so

⇨   Appoint someone to handle your finances should you be unable to do so

⇨   Arrange to pay for your health care should you need long term nursing care, including qualifying for MEDICAID.

⇨   Avoid Guardianship.

This book explains when and how to do all of these things. The book is written in plain English. It is intended for use by the average person.

Main   4/12